*The*

# ANATOMY

*of*

# INEQUALITY

# The
# ANATOMY
## *of*
# INEQUALITY

.

Its Social and Economic Origins—
and Solutions

———

# PER MOLANDER

TRANSLATED FROM THE SWEDISH BY SASKIA VOGEL

MELVILLE HOUSE
BROOKLYN · LONDON

# THE ANATOMY OF INEQUALITY

First Melville House Printing: August 2016

Melville House Publishing                    8 Blackstock Mews
            46 John Street         and       Islington
       Brooklyn, NY 11201                    London N4 2BT

mhpbooks.com    facebook.com/mhpbooks    @melvillehouse

Library of Congress Cataloging-in-Publication Data
Names: Molander, Per, author.
Title: The anatomy of inequality : its social and economic
    origins—and solutions / Per Molander ; translated from the
    Swedish by Saskia Vogel.
Other titles: Ojämlikhetens anatomi. English
Description: Brooklyn : Melville House, [2016] | "Originally
    published by Weyler Bokförlag [in 2014]." | Includes biblio-
    graphical references.
Identifiers: LCCN 2016016261 | ISBN 9781612195698
    (hardcover) | ISBN 9781612195704 (ebook)
Subjects: LCSH: Equality. | Income distribution. | Social
    stratification. | Economics—Sociological aspects.
Classification: LCC HM821 .M6513 2016 | DDC 305—dc23
LC record available at https://lccn.loc.gov/2016016261

*Design by Marina Drukman*

Printed in the United States of America
1   3   5   7   9   10   8   6   4   2

It is the common fate of the indolent to see their rights become a prey to the active. The condition upon which God hath given liberty to man is eternal vigilance.

—JOHN PHILPOT CURRAN,
Irish lawyer and politician, 1790

# CONTENTS

Preface     ix

1. Inequality and Its Shadow     3
2. Playing Marbles     11
3. The Archeology of Inequality     25
4. The End of the Tale     57
5. The Art of Flying     77
6. Back to the Social Contract     89
7. Liberalism and Inequality     113
8. Conservatism: Inequality as a
   Necessity and an Asset     133
9. Social Democracy and Inequality     163
10. Closing the Book     181

Notes     185
Bibliography     203

## PREFACE

This book began with a simple observation: virtually all human societies are marked by inequality, at a level that surpasses what could be expected from normal differences in individuals' capabilities alone. This observation—and my dissatisfaction with the fact that the social sciences have been either unable to come to grips with it or uninterested in doing so—is at the heart of *The Anatomy of Inequality*.

I first began to think about the ideas in this book around 1980, when I had finished my Ph.D. studies at the Department of Automatic Control at the University of Lund, in Sweden. Automatic control is a branch of applied mathematics devoted to the control of engineering systems and industrial processes—autopilots, nuclear power plants, etc. KarlJohan Åström, my mentor at the time, realized that unlike earlier graduates, I was not likely to enter the paper-and-pulp or robotics industries, so he suggested that I should learn economics.

I started with a title that appeared appropriate for someone with prior knowledge on optimization: *Mathematical Optimization and Economic Theory*, by the UCLA economist Michael Intriligator. The book's sixth chapter deals with game theory, including John Nash's theory of bargaining. Nash developed his mathematical theory of bargaining in the early 1950s and, many decades later, he was awarded the Prize in Economics in memory of Alfred Nobel for his work. An exercise toward the end of this chapter in Intriligator's book aims at testing whether the student masters Nash's solution to the bargaining game and carries the message that a wealthy person will gain more from a bilateral negotiation than will a poor person. The reflexes I had acquired during my studies of control theory were immediately aroused: here was an example of positive feedback, implying instability if the game of bargaining is repeated. If the wealthy person gets even wealthier from a round of bargaining, there is no mechanism that keeps the outcome within reasonable bounds. I expected to find a chapter discussing how to control this instability, but there was none. Remedying inequality was obviously not considered a worthy topic for economists, according to the author.

Three decades or so later, I finally found the time necessary to dig deeper into the problem of inequality, as well as into the social-science research devoted to it. There is a vast literature on both income inequality and social stratification—scientists such as Tony Atkinson, Amartya Sen, and more recently, Thomas Piketty have become known to a wider public—but the general focus of this work is on marginal change. Questions one typically encounters are why economic inequality is somewhat more pronounced in some liberal democracies than others, how the Gini coefficient of personal income distribution in a given country has developed over time, and so on. Following rising inequalities in developed countries during the latest three to four decades, economists even in institutions such as the Organisation for Economic Co-operation and Development (OECD) and the International Monetary Fund (IMF) have begun to look for driving forces behind this development. Yet relatively little energy has been spent on searching for fundamental mechanisms that generate inequality in a society.

This book, then, seeks to investigate how inequality of wealth and income can be expected to develop in a society with an egalitarian distribution of assets. This is not to say that all inequalities are arbitrary; there are differences in capabilities and efforts that explain some of the inequalities in status and wealth that we observe around the world. But the positive-feedback mechanism hinted at above—the wealthy person becomes even wealthier with every round of interaction—will lead to instability. If the original egalitarian distribution of wealth is disturbed, this disturbance will grow with time and will cause differences in outcomes to be completely out of proportion with differences in efforts or capabilities. The appropriate question is not "Why are all societies characterized by inequality?" but rather "Why have certain societies managed to keep inequality within reasonable bounds?" This, as I see it, is the origin of the universal political problem of wealth distribution.

What can a radically simplified theory—two parties bargaining with each other—tell us about complex power relations in human societies? A great deal, in my opinion—provided that the assumptions of the theory are general enough. Despite a number of challenges since its introduction in the 1950s, Nash's theory of bargaining has remained central to economic and philosophical discourse for decades. Still, a flaw of the model used in this book is its restriction to two parties. I was therefore pleased to see that only a month after the publication of the Swedish edition of the book, Ricardo and Robert Fernholz published a paper in the *Journal of Economic Dynamics and Control* that offered a similar analysis for a market. The conclusion is the same: even in a society where everyone starts with equal assets and capabilities and mobilizes the same effort, the distribution of wealth will eventually drive toward an extremely skewed distribution, in which a single household ends up owning everything.

In this book, I have combined a series of empirical observations with the basics of bargaining theory and a few other analytical tools. I have also confronted the main ideologies of the Western tradition—liberalism, conservatism, and socialism—with the conclusions of the analysis, in order to identify their relative strengths and weaknesses with respect to the complex of inequality. The discussion is general and often abstract, yet it is concrete enough, I believe, to permit rather sharp conclusions.

The thrust of *The Anatomy of Inequality* is descriptive and analytical, rather than normative. As a result, concepts such as *justice* and *fairness* are seldom used in the text. This is not because I believe them to be unimportant—both history and literature prove that they are not—but rather because a discussion of such concepts is more likely to be constructive if it is based on a thorough understanding of the processes that determine where a society will end up in terms of inequality. My experience from a whole working life as a policy analyst is that policy failures often stem from incomplete knowledge about the mechanisms at work. The story about the success of the Wright brothers, which appears in Chapter 5, lends credence to this view.

As I have mentioned, this book evolved over a fairly long period. Over the years, I have benefited from discussions with numerous colleagues and friends. Special thanks go to those whose comments on earlier drafts of the text helped to improve its presentation in various ways: Bengt Hansson, Rolf Johansson, Per Lekberg, Hannu Nurmi, Michael Sohlman, Ingolf Ståhl, Daniel Tarschys, Jörgen Weibull, and Gunnar Wetterberg. As always in these situations, the author is solely responsible for whatever flaws remain in the text.

*The*

# ANATOMY
*of*
# INEQUALITY

# 1

## INEQUALITY AND ITS SHADOW

*The social contract as a figure of thought has been
with us for more than two thousand years, and, clearly,
it is here to stay.*

Inequality has followed humankind throughout history. It has
left traces everywhere, which are excavated and examined by
archeologists.

A Sumerian hymn from Nippur, written in cuneiform
and translated in 1951, extols the goddess Nanshe:

> *Who knows the orphan, who knows the widow,
> knows the oppression of man over man, is the orphan's
> mother,
> Nanshe, who cares for the widow,
> who seeks out justice for the poorest.*

*The queen brings the refugee to her lap,*
*finds shelter for the weak.*

This fragment is four thousand years old, making it one of the oldest documents known to us. It speaks of oppression, of orphans and widows as representatives of oppressed groups. It also conveys a restrained discontent about the state of things—the text has a moral sounding box.

But it is not unique. The following lines, taken from a stele erected for an Egyptian bureaucrat at the start of the second millennium BCE, praise the same virtues:

*I was collected, kind, merciful,*
*who quieted the weeper with a kind word.*

[. . .]

*I was generous, open-handed,*
*a lord of provisions, free from neglect.*
*I was a friend to the little,*
*sweet of charm to the have-not.*
*I was the carer of the hungry who was without goods,*
*open-handed to the poor.*

Here again is an ancient account of inequality—and of an ethical norm that counterbalances it.

It was only in the 1900s that we began to approach an ideal of reasonable equality—universal suffrage, equality under the law (in principle), respect for personal integrity and fundamental material security. But this only applied to some parts of the world, and even then, the West saw a number of notable lapses into despotism that reversed this progress. Human history is essentially a history of inequality.

This degree of historical consistency over time—the omnipresence of inequality—warrants an explanation. But so does inequality's shadow: for millennia, the benchmark of equality has loomed just as large, if more abstractly, and it, too, deserves to be investigated. After all, the authors of the early accounts above were not only reacting to their surroundings—thousands of years ago, like many of their descendants today, they had a vision of a different society.

Can political philosophy help us understand the story of inequality—and of equality? Political philosophy explores what makes a good society. There are essentially three ways to pursue this philosophical inquiry. One approach—a relatively lazy one—is to use the status quo as a starting point and to discuss how best to manage it. A philosopher might then suggest some marginal changes to society, all of which would stem from the current state. Niccolò Machiavelli and David Hume are exponents of this philosophical method.

Another method is to begin with a sketch of a society, neither arguing for nor against various alternatives. *The Laws of Manu*, which outlines the Indian caste system, and Plato's *Republic* are examples from this tradition. These are not strictly works of political philosophy, however, because they avoid the question of how the proposed solution will gain legitimacy. Instead, they simply make reference to some historical mystery or shadow. Some more recent examples are Thomas More's *Utopia*, Tommaso Campanella's *The City of the Sun*, and Robert Owen's *A New View of Society*. The common feature of these blueprints is their level of detail: there are rules and regulations for all of life's eventualities, and even forays into urban planning.

The third and more purely philosophical tradition aims to first define rights and freedoms and then to establish, on this basis, a legitimate foundation for political power. In one of the most important traditions, creating a society is presented as a *social contract* in which a group of people give up some of their individual freedoms in order to share in the fruits of the community. The philosophical discussion, then, is about the terms of this contract.

No actual historical situation is described when employing this model of thought, even if there have been a few situations that have come close to resembling it. Nonetheless, it possesses a key strength: it clears the table of historical inheritance and other contingencies in order to discuss the terms from a perspective that, at the very least, has an egalitarian starting point, even if there is no guarantee of an egalitarian result. This approach is intellectually appealing; contract theories have been published at a fairly steady rate from classical antiquity to modern times. The first contributions come from the Greek philosophers, such as the Epicureans, the Cynics, and the Stoics—approaches that were systematized in the first century BCE by Lucretius in his work *On the Nature of Things*.

During the Middle Ages, the concept was given a Christian framework by Manegold of Lautenbach and Nicholas of Cusa. Marsilius of Padua was bold enough to discuss contracts in non-religious terms, and in doing so, he was far ahead of his time. Hugo Grotius and Thomas Hobbes were still writing within a religious framework in the 1600s, even if it was quite clear that to them God was an unnecessary hypothesis, and Jean-Jacques Rousseau's analysis of the social contract presaged the French Revolution.

The work of Hobbes and Rousseau provoked liberal responses. This was classical liberalism, rather than social liberalism, and its proponents—Bernard Mandeville, Adam Smith, John Stuart Mill, and others—did not write in terms of a social contract. Indeed, contemporary heirs to the tradition, such as Friedrich von Hayek, have declared their contempt for the concept as a whole. Still, their thoughts about society often revolve around a kind of ideal constitution—one of von Hayek's more prominent works is titled *The Constitution of Liberty*—so the approach is present, if unwittingly.

Although the idea of a social contract lost some of its appeal, particularly when it came under the scrutiny of conservative and right-leaning liberal critics, John Rawls's *A Theory of Justice* gave it new life during the 1970s, and when Robert Nozick launched a counterattack with *Anarchy, State, and Utopia* a few years later, he also argued using contractual terms, even though the content of his contract differed from that of Rawls's.

The social contract as a figure of thought has been with

us for more than two thousand years, and clearly, it is here to stay.

A remarkable amount of political philosophy has been written without the involvement of social scientists. This is a rather strange fact. If you take it upon yourself to discuss how people's relationships should be regulated in the political realm—whether that takes the form of a social contract or a constitution—the knowledge of how people actually behave in various situations should be key to any inquiry. Because politics by and large is about the division of a society's immaterial and material resources—and because any overview of the history of humankind cannot help but leave one with the overwhelming impression that these resources have been inequitably divided—the most reasonable starting point for a discussion is an analysis of the mechanisms of inequality. Then the central question becomes "Why are all societies unequal?"

A logical follow-up question that naturally emerges from this first one is: "Can inequality be politically influenced?" Conservatives often assert that precisely *because* inequality is a common trait of nearly every society, one should perhaps avoid trying to influence the distribution of life chances, incomes, and assets. Yet this is a hasty conclusion to draw. Even if inequality cannot be eliminated, the level of inequality and its structure and degree might be open to political influence, and in this way, be kept within reasonable bounds.

A third question is how the main alternatives described in

the classical ideologies—liberalism, conservatism, socialism—address inequality as a phenomenon. An ideology, after all, is a kind of map that helps us orient ourselves on the political landscape. If, then, inequality is one of the fundamental problems in politics, a critical assessment of how it is described and influenced within these ideological frameworks is essential if one wants to determine their validity.

# 2

## PLAYING MARBLES

*You can . . . ask how much better than the rich
person does the poor person have to be at playing the
game to have as great a chance of winning . . .*

A common explanation of ubiquitous inequality is that people
differ with respect to capability and effort. This is inadequate
as an explanation of the differences that we actually observe,
however. The British organization Oxfam showed in a report
that in 2015, the eighty richest persons in the world owned
as much as the poorer half of the world's population, about
3.5 billion people. That this gap in assets, corresponding to
a factor of 10 to 100 million, should be explained by differences in productivity and effort is a physical impossibility. A
day and night comprises twenty-four hours for all of us, and
in the poorer half of the world's population one finds a large
number of reasonably well-educated persons from middle-
income countries.

Another explanation sometimes put forward is that differences have been created and maintained by the use of violence. Indeed many cultural encounters have been characterized by violence, in many cases without restraint. But in these encounters, one of parties was often inferior already at the outset. Further, violence is a costly method of maintaining social structures, and periods of active violence have been relatively short in relation to human history as a whole. Threats of violence may sometimes be sufficient, but then we are already in a different regime.

As will be seen in the following chapter, older social structures in human history are often more equal, even if they do not reach the limit ideal of social contract theories. There is need for a mechanism that explains why inequality rises and is reinforced over time. Here is a key to understanding:

> On the square one day a little boy and I
> played marbles.
>
> I had around thirty, and he had three.
> And as we played he lost them to me.
>
> He snuffled and sniveled and gave me a stare,
> I smirked and walked off with nary a care
>
> But when I came home, I had my regrets,
> I had done something wrong, but I might right it yet.

*I sprinted back, but there was no one around*
*who could say where that schoolboy was to be found.*

*I was ashamed. I think I am still,*
*when I watch them playing marbles so well.*

*And what I would give to someday see*
*that boy—just once—filled with glee.*

*But somewhere now he's a large and rough man,*
*who drudges and toils for the rest of his span.*

*Even if I found him, that time has gone.*
*You can't rewind and right an old wrong.*

*You can't return marbles from way back when*
*and comfort the boys who've hardened to men.*

—STEN SELANDER, "Playing Marbles"

As children, most of us will have experienced something similar to what Sten Selander's poem describes, either in the role of the poem's narrator, or as the little boy. We are transported back to that moment, and we will either recall the sweet victory, or the bitter loss. The victor might experience a gnawing feeling that the win had more to do with luck than anything else, but that feeling will soon recede. For the loser, the game offers something darker: a lesson in coping with the inevitable disappointments of adult life.

But let us return to the results of the game: Did the right player win? For some, this question is nonsensical: of course the right player won. He won all the marbles, and thus he must have been the better player. But this statement is problematic. When the game began, the conditions for each player were not the same: "I guess I had thirty, and he had three." As with so many other things in life, there is an element of chance in the game of marbles. If two equally talented players meet, and one has thirty marbles and the other has three, who has the greatest chance of winning? The rules state that the game ends when one of the players has lost all of his marbles.

To attain an answer, we must turn to a mathematical tool called a Markov chain, yet that answer can be formulated simply, without getting bogged down in complex analysis. If both players are equally skilled and one player has ten times as many marbles as the other, he will be ten times as likely to win. This means that, on average, he will win in more than nine out of ten cases, whereas the other player will win fewer than one in ten times.

These results have nothing to do with skill or effectiveness. After all, we are assuming that both players are equally skilled. The one who has the most marbles when the game begins will most likely win *because he has the most marbles.*

This is just one example of the many self-reinforcing mechanisms in our lives. It is easy to imagine how a person rich in marbles might tour the city playing the game, continuously increasing his holdings—unless of course he has the rotten luck of meeting someone with one hundred marbles when he happens to be down to only sixty or seventy.

You can turn the problem around: how much better does the poor person have to be to have as great a chance of winning one game of marbles? The answer: about 26 percent better.

This simple scene contains the building blocks for an explanation of how inequality can arise even in a society so enlightened and lucky that talent, industriousness, and external material prerequisites are all equally distributed. Small deviations from total equality will increase with time. If property and assets can be inherited, inequality will also intensify from generation to generation.

The game of marbles can also serve as a starting point for a political discussion. Does the game have to be played by these rules? No, of course it does not. You could restrict the game in any number of ways: both players could only play, for example, if each of them had three marbles at the beginning—no more, no less. They would then have the same chance of winning, as long as they are equally skilled. You could also shift the focus of the game, making it less about winning and more about developing players' skills. Everyone could walk away from the game with as many marbles as they had when the game began. They would be better players, but not more unequal ones.

Those who already have many marbles might offer a tautological objection that the person with the most marbles has more marbles because he is, in fact, more skilled. This might be true in certain situations, but even a cursory glance at ac-

tual inequalities will show that it is an insufficient explanation. Generally speaking, neither historic nor present-day
differences in income or wealth are proportional to differences
in talent or effort. We must also consider that the social exchanges that determine who gets what may nurture traits that
we do not necessarily want to nurture, such as recklessness,
aggression, and mendacity.

Success in competition is not always determined by the
traits or behavioral patterns that we would prefer to associate with success. This is an insight that many find difficult to
grasp—and even more difficult to internalize. We computed
for the game of marbles that given the imbalance of assets at
the start, the poorer player has to be 26 percent more skillful
in order to stand an equal chance of winning. This implies that
if he is 20 percent better, he will most likely not win. Natural
selection will not favor the best player.

In wider social discourse, it is not uncommon to hear arguments that come dangerously close to the optimistic fanta-
sies voiced by Dr. Pangloss in Voltaire's *Candide*—that we live
in the best of all possible worlds. But the things that occur in
the market are not always the most beneficial for the whole,
even when ethical considerations are removed from the equa-
tion. "Does the fittest necessarily survive?" asked the economist Martin Shubik in a 1954 article. His conclusion was in
the negative, and he explained why using a duel as his example. If two gunmen meet in a duel, the one with the greatest
likelihood of hitting the other is also most likely to win. But if
the number of gunmen is increased to three, this statement is

already rendered false. If three men meet for a three-way gun-fight—everyone against everyone else—and two of them have a greater chance of hitting the other than the third does, then the best strategy for these two is to fight each other, which means that the third—the least skilled—ends up with the greatest chance of surviving.

We often assume that the Panglossian idea might at least apply to biology, where everything that occurs seems to serve a greater purpose, or at least expresses what we think should be decisive: the ability to find food, speed, strength, and the like. Yet sexual reproduction, for example, is governed by a number of factors, some of which do not favor strength. One behavioral pattern that comes close to echoing Shubik's duelists is what the ecologist John Maynard Smith calls *sneaky fuckers*: males who take the opportunity to breed with a female as two larger, stronger males are busy fighting over that very female.

In certain species—elephant seals, for example—the females are mounted by a small number of males who, relative to their strength, disproportionately dominate the act of breeding. Over the course of a season in an elephant-seal colony, fewer than one-third of all males have the chance to mate, and many males leave no (or almost no) genetic imprint because they either die before they reach sexual maturity or have been eliminated in competition. This is a pattern that favors the genes responsible for aggression—that is why they are there—but it does not necessarily favor the flock or the species, and it certainly does not favor the males who never get a chance to pass on their genetic material.

Other behavioral patterns that can lead to success in nature and in society involve trickery and deception, rather than survival of the fittest, objectively speaking. Harmless species sometimes survive by imitating more dangerous species through *mimicry*, to use the biological term. Lies and deception are constant threats to human relationships, in spite of comprehensive countermeasures like verification processes, testimonials, and stamps of authenticity. Examples are manifold.

## Negotiation Is Necessary

But life consists of more than marbles, duels, and sex. More clearly dominant elements in the social exchange need to be identified. One of these elements is *negotiation*. Exchange in various forms is fundamental to every human interaction. Certain thinkers have even wanted to posit exchange as a social equivalent to chemical bonds: fundamental relationships on which more complex social structures are built. The sociologist Émile Durkheim believed exchange to be the basis for social solidarity.

An exchange as old as humankind itself takes place between parents and their children. With their parents' help, children learn to walk, speak, control their defecation, and socialize in groups. As children grow up, they encounter the division of labor—along the lines of age, gender, etc. Every division of labor presupposes that a negotiation took place, either explicitly or implicitly. If one person does one thing and another person does something else, then it must be determined how much is fair to ask of the other in return. Parents have always taken care of their offspring during childhood. In return, when those parents become unable to care for themselves, children are expected to care for them. What can parents demand? Similarly, women and men divide certain tasks between them in most societies, even if the divisions themselves vary greatly from society to society. What is a reasonable division? To answer all of these questions, negotiation is necessary.

In everyday language, we mainly use the word *negotiation* when establishing prices, wages, and other terms, as in the case of a salesman who tries to convince a customer that she cannot live without a certain product, while the customer tries to drive down the price by feigning disinterest. Such negotiation games are also common in politics, when, for example, a government is being formed, or when international trade agreements are being drafted.

Tourists who haggle at a bazaar in a foreign country might enjoy the process itself, and political negotiations can also have symbolic value in public opinion. But in most cases, the time and energy spent on a negotiation amount to a burden. The seller and the buyer might have rules of thumb that help them arrive at their final terms—last month's price, the price at another nearby market, possibly complemented by information about changes in their surroundings. If such information is not available, the parties are likely to simply meet in the middle.

In many modern markets, negotiations have completely disappeared. No one haggles over the price of a loaf of bread at a grocery store; you either accept the price and go through with the transaction, or you hold off and perhaps go to another store. Within the family, parents and children often have different understandings of how responsibilities and tasks should be divided, but no negotiations take place, because both parties can guess what the result will be. In working life, there are many examples of tasks that are allocated in ways that do not require much discussion, even if the affected employees might harbor unvoiced opinions about how the tasks should be divided.

But open negotiations have not completely disappeared from the market. Home prices are often arrived at after drawn-out negotiations between the buyer and the seller, and even the price of mass-produced products, like cars, can be negotiable, especially if next year's model is around the corner and the seller is stuck with unsold lots of last year's model. How compelling open negotiations can be depends, of course, on the value of what is at stake and what the negotiation itself will cost in time and effort.

But even if open negotiation continues to apply in certain realms, the prevailing relationships of exchange (whether they involve the price of a product or the distribution of responsibility within a family) tend to mirror an underlying power relationship. Just because the formal process is not visible does not mean that a harmony of interests reigns.

# A Long History

Adam Smith begins the second chapter of *The Wealth of Nations* (1776) with the following observation on the division of labor and negotiations:

> This division of labour, from which so many advantages are derived, is not originally the effect of any human wisdom, which foresees and intends that general opulence to which it gives occasion. It is the necessary, though very slow and gradual, consequence of a certain propensity in human nature, which has in view no such extensive utility; the propensity to truck, barter, and exchange one thing for another.
>
> Whether this propensity be one of those original principles in human nature, of which no further account can be given, or whether, as seems more probable, it be the necessary consequence of the faculties of reason and speech, it belongs not to our present subject to inquire. It is common to all men, and to be found in no other race of animals, which seem to know neither this nor any other species of contracts.

You might agree with Smith that the origins of negotiation have been lost to an unknown pre-history. Still, it seems reasonable to view negotiation as an inevitable consequence of the division of labor, rather than the other way around. For the entirety of the archeological record, trade has been carried about by people—metal tools traded for fur, food traded for jewelry, and so on. Agricultural development and the social stratification that followed created new, imbalanced negotiation situations—between landowners and farmworkers, between landowners and lease-holders, and eventually between leaders with better- or worse-equipped armed forces.

Negotiations have not been limited to exchanges of goods and services. Marriages have typically been entered into after comprehensive negotiations over a bartered bride or a wedding dowry. Anthropologists have determined that particular forms dominate in particular conditions: bartered brides, for example, are mostly found in small-scale, male-dominated societies where polygamy is allowed.

Gift-giving is a form of exchange that has interested many anthropologists, including Marcel Mauss, Bronislaw Malinowski, and others. At the start of his classic monograph *The Gift*, Mauss establishes that in many societies, gifts are only voluntary in theory, and that in reality, both the giving of gifts and giving them in return is comparable to a duty. He notes that it is also often the case that groups, rather than individuals, are the parties in these exchanges, agreements, and obligations. In the societies in the South Pacific that Mauss was studying, not giving a gift when one was expected to, not sending an invitation, or declining an invitation was tantamount to a declaration of war. So the purpose of gifts and invitations was to create social cohesion and prevent conflict.

In his book *Argonauts of the Western Pacific*, Malinowski studied the Kula ring, a sophisticated system of exchange conducted across the Trobriand Islands in Melanesia. The Kula ring was built on two items of trade (bracelets and necklaces) that were circulated in two streams—around the islands counterclockwise and clockwise, respectively. The trade presupposed reciprocity; it was important that gifts and gifts-in-return were of the same value. Furthermore, the gifts-in-return should arrive with some delay, so that a system of debt was cultivated, which also strengthened social cohesion. Every exchange was preceded by a negotiation.

The modern gift economy—Christmas presents in the Christian part of the world and Diwali gifts in Indian society, to take two examples—has much in common with premodern institutions. Even if the formal framework has been abandoned in many situations, the underlying rules are generally understood, and a breach of these rules might lead to mistrust or even conflict.

The act of negotiation has been with us since the dawn of man. Durkheim, Mauss, and the other classical thinkers correctly observed that exchange is a fundamental bonding agent in social structures. Negotiation is not confined to what we in modern society call the economic sphere. It occurs in all facets of life, and it endures in older forms in areas that are still relatively untouched by market forces. Negotiations, more or less implicit, are the life-blood of the economic sphere, and the forces of the market have found their way into even the finest capillaries of civic life. Negotiations also determine, more or less, the political sphere's labor conditions. To understand the mechanisms that create inequality, it is necessary to understand the dynamics of negotiation. First, an overview of the landscape of inequality—historically and globally—will be given.

# 3

## THE ARCHEOLOGY OF INEQUALITY

*When taking a long historical view, we see a clear
tendency towards rising inequality.*

A historical perspective of inequalityrequires a map of the terrain, and ideally a tool for measuring it. People's resources can vary in a number of ways—income, assets, intellectual ability, social status, sexual privilege—and high status in one area is no guarantee of high status in another.

To get a relatively precise picture of the way things are, it is desirable to summarize the distribution of assets with a single measure. Sociologists, economists, and statisticians have been developing such measures for a long time and have reached something of a consensus on which is the most suitable. Deciding on the best measure to use depends on the question in focus—a general description of development over time, for instance, or the contemporary position of those with the most hardship or wealth.

Historical descriptions of inequality vary in precision and quality. The branch of the evolutionary tree that eventually becomes modern humans diverged from its closest primate relatives about six million years ago. Following that split, the archeological record has been sparse, by and large. We have to rely on reconstructions and rough indicators. The archeological evidence is strongly biased toward buildings and objects made of stone and metal, typical status symbols that are more likely to endure than objects made of less hardy materials.

For most of recorded history, we only have imprecise evaluations and qualified guesses at our disposal. The sizes of dwellings can be reconstructed from excavations, and average income can be deduced from the quantity of grain in certain areas and time periods, but on the whole, the picture is murky. Only with the introduction of tax rolls and censuses as tools for the administration of the nation-state did it become possible to describe more accurately the distribution of income and resources.

It should be noted that even with the fairly detailed data available on industrialized countries today, inequality remains a feature of statistical distributions. As soon as you condense distribution into a single number, like a Gini coefficient or a statistical standard deviation, information is lost. Inequality can indeed fluctuate without the fluctuation being reflected in these numbers. And so every succinct assertion about distribution must be understood to be a simplification.

But distribution is not only about income and resources. Other fundamental aspects of welfare include freedom of movement, equality before the law, and access to basic services like education and healthcare, and every thorough description of the distribution of welfare should include these elements. If such statistics are available, as they often are in industrialized countries, the question arises of how these elements are to be aggregated into a single measure. The answer will necessarily depend on valuations.

The most frequently used measure in modern research is the Gini coefficient, also known as the Gini index, which was developed by the Italian sociologist and statistician Corrado Gini in the early 1900s. The Gini coefficient is best described as a number that expresses the distance between the actual distribution of income or wealth and a completely equal distribution. Put another way: in an income distribution with a given average income, the Gini index is a measure of the expected difference in income between two randomly selected individuals.

A Gini coefficient is a score between 0 and 1; it is 0 if income distribution is completely equal and 1 if all income or wealth is held by a single person. In OECD-member countries, the coefficient typically varies between 0.2 and 0.4. Countries like Brazil and Namibia, meanwhile, have much higher scores (between 0.6 and 0.7, or higher).

It is important to keep in mind that the Gini coefficient is a number that can obscure quite varied distributions. You can get different results depending on what you measure— individuals or households. The reason for measuring by household is that a redistribution within the household occurs that evens out the opportunities for consumption. That said, in many cultures great differences prevail between men and women in the same household, which puts the usefulness of the household as entity unit in question.

Income-distribution figures are most commonly made available, but in some cases it might be more important to show the distribution of *assets*. Assets are often less equally distributed than income, because people with higher incomes do not need to spend as great a share of their earnings. Just how unequally assets are distributed depends on what is included; if real estate is included, the distribution is more even, but many people do not consider real estate investments to be on a par with stocks and bank assets.

## Our Closest Relatives

Biology has been used and abused in philosophy and politics, as is tragically evidenced in twentieth-century history. This discussion is not normative, but descriptive, however, and facts derived from research into primate behavior can help broaden our frames of reference—though, naturally, there are some caveats.

You might be wondering how literature on primate behavior is relevant to a discussion about equality. Indeed, what is true for chimpanzees or gorillas is not necessarily true for humans. Such an objection is justified, but it must be weighed against the benefit of expanding the frame of reference. To illustrate how the distribution of influence and resources affects everyday problems, it is enough that we share some general traits. It has been shown that game theory's models of cooperation and conflict can be applied to a wide variety of species in the animal kingdom, because once the superficial differences have been stripped away, the basic structure of everyday decision-making is the same.

In addition, the age-old notion—religious in origin—that humans are unique creatures has been challenged with increasing intensity in recent decades, and the notion that only humans use tools was dispelled long ago. The more modest version of this assertion—that humans distinguish themselves by *making* tools—does not stand, since it has been proven that chimpanzees also make tools, of their own accord and without any training. As for language, apes do have the ability to manipulate symbols, even if opinions on their syntactic skills are divided. Chimpanzees have a sense of identity and can recognize themselves in the mirror and on film. Not only do they have a sense of self, but they also have a sense of The Other, and the current consensus is that higher-status apes have a grasp of concepts and thinking; they can take on another chimpanzee's point of view. They can also plan—imagining objects that are not there and future events and choosing courses of action that are not motivated by short-term utility. Whether or not that should be called *reason* is a matter of definition.

Ethologists have long debated the relative value of studying free versus captive chimpanzees. In studies of apes in zoos, there is a risk that the observed behavioral patterns are influenced by the artificial environment. On the other hand, this environment allows for much more detailed observations of chains of events and causality than studies conducted in a natural environment. As Frans de Waal has pointed out, all the behaviors that he and his colleagues have observed in captive apes—more than one hundred behavioral patterns in all—are also observed in the wild. Restricted space gives rise to aggressive behavior, but as long as an animal's domain is sizable, the behaviors being observed are, in fact, natural.

Inequality does arise between chimps, and it is complex. In contrast to chickens, which have a simple pecking order, chimpanzees tend to live in networks. The leader is always male, usually a strong male, but not necessarily the strongest, physically. Chimpanzees have a certain ability to organize themselves hierarchically in order to efficiently perpetrate large-scale acts of violence. They can coordinate hunting expeditions, and when in conflict with other groups of apes, the dominant males might force the other males to join them in battle. But within the group, the strength of each individual ape determines the extent of what can be achieved. Males are stronger than females on average, but two or three females are usually stronger than a male.

Consequently, coalitions are essential to a leader who wishes to keep hold of his power. The alpha male is usually supported by other males (who are weaker, for the time being), but he cannot ignore the wishes of females and juveniles without jeopardizing his rank. The support of other males carries with it the seeds of perfidy if they have designs on becoming the leader themselves. And so the leader needs to employ classic techniques, which we know from human politics: the formation of new coalitions, manipulation, dividing and conquering.

The alpha male lives under permanent stress because he must constantly reassert his dominance. If he does not fit the bill for the position he has reached in some way, he has to manipulate the others into believing that he deserves that position; bluffing and making noise are forms of manipulation. The leader will constantly try to verify that his authority is not in question, and other members of the group will satisfy this wish by performing symbolic acts of submission and other ritualized behaviors. But the reigning power structure is always vulnerable, because changes in coalitions can undermine it in no time. In those cases, the shift in power can be dramatic.

How a leader distributes resources and resolves conflict can help strengthen his legitimacy. If a group suddenly gains access to something valuable, like a bunch of bananas, the leader will immediately try to monopolize this resource, only to share it with the group in order to gain respect for his generosity. When there is greater access to food that needs to be found and that requires a group effort to do so, as is the norm in a natural habitat, such demonstrations of power are not possible, and this leads to more-equal power dynamics within the group.

All groups will enter into conflict at some point. In these situations, it is the leader's duty to prevent the conflict from getting worse and, if possible, to resolve it. However, conflict resolution is not the leader's exclusive privilege; groups of females often serve a function in conflict management and have even been observed disarming aggressive males.

Power and sexuality have a strong correlation. A powerful social position confers sexual benefits, and the leader jealously guards these privileges from other males. Females have a certain freedom of action, and having power does not automatically lead to popularity among females. In fact, it is difficult for a male to keep a female from having sex against his will.

More generally, social status and influence over the group are not one and the same. Personality matters in the small communities in which chimps live. Successfully establishing good relations with females seems to be an important factor in exerting influence over the group as a whole.

Behavioral researchers have long discussed whether or not primates have an inherent tendency to seek power, or if power is simply a tool used to attain material and social goals. In the 1930s, the behaviorist Abraham Maslow coined the term *dominance drive*, but many ethologists were skeptical. Now, leading researchers such as Frans de Waal and Jane Goodall are convinced; their observations have confirmed that chimpanzees sometimes make material sacrifices to gain power. Hobbes's assumptions in the introduction to *Leviathan* seem apposite to the discussion:

> So that in the first place, I put for a general in-
> clination of all mankind a perpetual and rest-

less desire of power after power, that ceaseth
only in death. And the cause of this is not always that a man hopes for a more intensive de-
light than he has already attained to, or that he
cannot be content with a moderate power, but
because he cannot assure the power and means
to live well, which he hath present, without the
acquisition of more.

## Hunters, Gatherers, and Farmers

Every reconstruction of prehistoric hunter-gatherer societies
suffers from the fact that the archeological record is scant and
there are no written source materials. Most commonly, conclusions have been based on modern anthropological studies,
mostly conducted during the 1900s, operating on the assumption that the societies being studied resembled their prehistoric
predecessors. This is, at best, a risky assumption. Societies of
this kind that have lasted into modern times have their own
histories, and it is unlikely that their members' lives today are
much the same as they were a millennium or more ago. There
is reason to believe that history has left a deeper mark on these
societies than on those of our closest primate relatives. Nonetheless it is reasonable to assume that similar problems lead
to similar solutions, and modern hunter-gatherer societies can
be used as a first-order approximation. And so, with a bit of

daring, one can draw lines of development backward (toward primates) and forward (toward historical societies) to trace a general trajectory of human development.

*Hunter-gatherer societies* have traditionally been seen as models. Classical anthropologists like Edward Evans-Pritchard, Marshall Sahlins, and Elman Service described these societies as relatively healthy, peaceful, and egalitarian, but in later years, this rosy picture has been modified. Early descriptions tended to overstate the level of cooperation and the lack of hierarchy and leadership, while understating the level of aggression. Still, the generalization probably stands that men were more cooperative in these societies, the differences in status were less pronounced, and decisions were made more collectively than in settled societies and in the primate societies with which we are familiar.

The transition from nomadic life to a settled agricultural society did not happen in one fell swoop. Methods of stockpiling food were developed over long periods of time. Moveable homes were replaced with seasonal settlements. Running parallel to this development were indications of a rise in prestige and power. Studies from around the world suggest that there were growing social differences in the late paleolithic and mesolithic eras—that is, several tens of thousands of years ago—that have left their mark in the form of valuable objects, storage facilities controlled by individuals, and more. Olga Soffer has given an account of hunter-gatherer adaptations on the Upper Paleolithic central Russian plains, from 18,000 to 10,000 BCE. It was, in short, an economy of survival based on storage. Societies like these were less mobile than classical nomadic cultures. Diminished mobility reduced the individual's freedom of action and increased the opportunities to control labor and other limited resources. Even in the early period, the strengthening of hierarchies was expressed through differences in burial rites and in the size of houses. Depositories for bones, tusks, and food seem to have been more than just storage; they were instruments of power. In the later part of the period, hierarchical tendencies increased in the region. Monumental architecture (or at least what counted as monumental at the time) and exotic luxury goods are evidence of increasing social stratification.

Per Lekberg offers a similar perspective in his analysis of a large number of stone axes from the early Stone Age (2350 to 1700 BCE) in central Sweden, from which he drew conclusions about the distribution of wealth and social structures. The axes have been categorized by length, degree of fragmentation and wear, and whether their raw material—the blank—was found or extracted from a quarry. These combined factors determined the value of the axe for its owner. At some point, many of these axes broke near the shaft-hole and were recycled and repurposed into newer, smaller axes. And so the original raw material went through stages of gradual shortening until it was no longer useful—and followed its owner to the grave.

Axes have been found in graves, domiciles, and storehouse ruins. The variations in the axes' features are not random; they correspond to where they were found, which makes it possible to reconstruct the social landscape of the time. The most valuable axes were found in wealthy areas characterized by higher population density and larger homes. Findings from the later part of the period show that prosperity was concentrated. Lekberg links his interpretations to the social stratification that emerged in other parts of Europe at the time. He describes the stone axes and the environment in which they were being used as a sort of local dialect of the European Bronze Age's culture.

Farming presupposes settlement, but rooted ways of life developed independently of farming. Settlements make it possible to accumulate and transmit wealth between generations and can therefore be expected to lead to increased inequality. One American study measured the efficiency of the intergenerational transmission of wealth, which includes knowledge, material resources, and networks. For hunter-gatherer societies, low to medium-high Gini coefficients—between 0.2 and 0.5—were found for all three resources. This is because the intergenerational transmission is moderate, but enough to have an impact on an individual's chances in life. Even in these societies, it matters who your parents are.

*Horticultural societies* rely on small-scale, low-intensity production of agricultural crops supplemented by fishing, hunting, and other types of foraging. High mobility, limited storage space, and small communities are factors that should lead to egalitarian horticultural societies. However, the Gini coefficient for these societies is quite high, even though intergenerational transmission is low. The conclusion is that it is not farming itself that leads to an increase in inequality, but the restriction of key resources that can be controlled and monopolized.

In *pastoral societies*, the transmission of wealth between generations is greater, particularly as it pertains to material resources. There are several contributing factors: economies of scale in herding; gifts and family inheritance; and the exploitation of networks related to marriage, accidents, and other significant events. Networks are particularly important when a society suffers a drought: a wealthy family would be able to borrow more to see the period through, for example. The Gini coefficient for these societies is typically between 0.4 and 0.5, but in extreme cases it can approach 0.7. In a general study of nearly 200 societies, slavery was shown to be rather common.

The domestication of animals, creating pastures for grazing, and the cultivation of crops—including tilling the land (sowing crops, harvesting, and storing seeds)—were big steps toward establishing an *agricultural society*. What spurred this development on has been much disputed—most likely, there were internal and external factors (the climate, for instance) at play, and the relative importance of assorted factors varied from area to area where the transition to farming was in progress. An important internal factor was the impulse to increase the concentration of power in the upper levels of society—in other words, among those who had a personal interest in steering development in this direction. The results were unambiguous, though: in agricultural societies, people increasingly faced contracting contagious diseases, had shorter average life spans, and were increasingly subjected to social conflicts.

When agriculture was well established, society became increasingly complex and stratified. The division of labor continued to evolve, and new jobs—such as merchant, craftsman, and administrator—were created. Agriculture indirectly contributed to strengthening hierarchies by increasing the need for a coordinated military defense. War was not unknown among hunter-gatherer societies—it is depicted in ten-thousand-year-old Australian cave paintings—but concentrated settlements with stores of food and livestock were of course attractive targets for nearby nomads plotting to carry out raids. Organized resistance against such raids, which included building fortifications, catalyzed the emergence of centralized social structures and further divisions of labor—in particular, specialists in armed combat. Once established, military forces could also be used against the people they were meant to protect—thereby undermining a fragile power balance based on a relatively even distribution of the capacity for violence.

Cities in a modern sense first sprung up in the Near East—Jericho and Çatal Höyük are the most famous examples. Urbanization fostered the ongoing processes of division of labor, social control, and stratification.

The first emergence of states is as disputed as the origin of agriculture. Like agriculture, states arose independently around the world—in Mesopotamia, the Mediterranean, and Egypt in the 3000s BCE, in the Indus Valley and China in the next millennium, and in Central and South America in the following millennium. No single factor or combination of factors can explain this emergence entirely, but there are a few shared traits: division of labor, control of key resources, and a monopoly on organized violence.

Farming intensified, and a surplus was created that freed certain people from having to work the land. This made room for specialized trades—qualified craftsmen, bureaucrats, and priests. States presuppose labor, and indeed, the classic trio of plough, sword, and book covers the main categories.

The historian Karl Wittfogel suggested that the need for a highly developed irrigation system aided the rise of despotism, but later investigations into Wittfogel's examples have challenged the validity of his theory as a general explanation. Nevertheless, those who control a resource as essential as water have a potentially huge capacity to wield power over others, so Wittfogel's theory does contain a kernel of truth.

Early states show some of the most extreme levels of inequality in history. A regent (often relatively successful in claiming divine right) was supported by a clergy, a central bureaucracy, and an army in his rule over large masses of farmers and their households as well as over landless farmworkers. The only limits those leaders placed on their concentration of power and resources were designed to ensure that agricultural workers would stay alive. Concessions also emerged when leaders encountered practical limitations to exercising their power, which was especially important in remote parts of a country at a time when transport and communications networks had not yet developed.

Using the same measuring techniques that were used to determine the Gini coefficient for hunter-gatherer and transitional societies, it has been established that this measure varies broadly for agricultural societies—between 0.2 and 0.7.

Material resources are now the most important factor in overall prosperity, and intergenerational transmission also plays a significant role.

In summary, the idea that inequality has increased throughout humankind's journey from simple hunter-gatherer societies to the polities at the edge of the historical era is corroborated. An essential part of the explanation lies in the gradual strengthening of the material element of welfare and the fact that this element is also the easiest to pass on from one generation to the next. But this particular development also saw many fits and starts, as is true for the rest of history.

## Early Historical and Classical Ages

Early polities were like modern states in that they relied on administration and trade. Both administration and trade contributed to the advancement of the art of writing—cuneiform in Mesopotamia, hieroglyphs in Egypt, and an Indian alphabet in the Indus Valley in the 3000s and 2000s BCE, and later Hittite hieroglyphs, the Aegean Linear B alphabet, the Phoenician alphabet, and Chinese characters in the next millennium. Greek and Brahmi scripts as well as Central American characters emerged even later. Certain systems emerged independently, while others had outside influences.

Most early texts are rather quotidian registries of administrative facts or economic transactions. For a long time, reading and writing was a secret well kept by the bureaucratic elite and contributed to articulating existing differences in society. But as the Sumerian and Egyptian extracts in Chapter 1 suggest, literature as we know it today eventually emerged, and it expressed norms that went against the interests of the ruling class. The political effect of this literature was of course limited.

Through the historiography that developed in Greece and Rome, we have more information about these societies than those that preceded them. Still, it is difficult to get a detailed picture of the living conditions and wealth distribution at the time. It has been estimated that the richest 8 to 9 percent of the population of Athens owned 30 to 35 percent of the land. Even by modern standards, this is rather an even distribution. Another interesting figure is that between 5 and 10 percent of Athenians were literate, also quite a high percentage.

But of course, democratic Athens had its blemishes. Slavery was widespread, and slaves, along with women and immigrants, were excluded from political life. Many slaves were prisoners of war; others were Athenians who were forced into bonded labor after they could not pay their rent. If the land was fully mortgaged, the only security left to offer was the body itself, which led to local slavery or, in the worst case, slavery abroad.

The Athens of the 500s played host to one of history's greatest bids for material redistribution: the reforms of Solon. This, in itself, is an indication of just how unequal the distribution of wealth was then. Solon's program for debt forgiveness was to remove the boundary stones (horoi) that indicated land that was being farmed by a person who was indebted to the large landowners. This would free those who had been enslaved because of debt, and forbid people's bodies from being used as lien for a loan. Solon also strove to bring back the Athenians who had been sold into slavery abroad, but it is not known to what extent he succeeded. The problem remained: how would small landowners support themselves? If the cultivated parcel of land was too small to support a household, writing off the debt would not help. Solon also regulated the market for all agricultural products (except olives), which strengthened the consumer's position but did not benefit modest, self-sufficient households.

There are earlier records of social reforms from the Middle East. In the city of Lagash, power was seized by one Urukagina at the middle of the third millennium BCE, who liberated its population from a corrupt administration and restored a more egalitarian distribution of assets. Exactly how far this debt relief was carried, and what the long-term effects were, is difficult to judge.

Jewish regulation related to the Jubilee year (from Leviticus 25) offers another early example of mitigating inequality—albeit a less concrete one. Every fifty years, all pawned property would be returned to its original owners (verse 13), and all slaves and their families would be freed (verse 54). Exceptions were made for property in cities (verse 30), indicating that the urban elite was behind the design of the program. Contrary to what we know about Solon's reforms, there is no evidence that these regulations were ever implemented.

The Gini coefficient for income distribution in classical Rome is thought to have been between 0.37 and 0.4. This might seem low, in that it corresponds with the number for the United States today, but there were so few extremely rich people in classical times (at least as far as we know) that they did not have a notable impact on income distribution.

Famine, as best we know, was uncommon in ancient Greece and Rome. Some serious periods of famine in Athens were recorded, but these were the result of sieges. Both Athens and Rome relied on imported grain, but it seems the authorities were well aware of the political risks involved, and they implemented successful emergency measures. One of Julius Caesar's final rulings before he was murdered was to rebuild Carthage—which had been destroyed a century before in the Punic Wars—as one of the Roman Empire's vital sources for grain.

In conclusion, classical societies—including Athens, which was a democratic and relatively egalitarian exception—were characterized by significant inequality. Life was fraught with problems for most citizens. From the beginning of history through the classical epoch, life for the majority of the population for most people in this time span was a struggle for survival.

## The Middle Ages

The availability of data on income and wealth in the Middle Ages is not much better than that for the previous historical period. There are some detailed records, including the English

*Domesday Book*, William the Conqueror's land registry from the late 1000s, but most of our knowledge is based on qualitative descriptions.

A few general observations can be drawn from the available data. First, Western Europe's population in 1000 was as large as it was in the year 0. Modern societies may be experiencing a demographic equilibrium with a stable population at a high material level, but this was not the case in medieval Europe. Second, the gross domestic product per person in Western Europe dropped between the years 0 and 1000 at a rate of 0.1 percent per year. This number does not tell us anything about the distribution of wealth, but there is no reason to believe that living conditions changed for the better during this long period of negative growth.

Life expectancy at birth does say something about the living conditions. In Egypt during the Roman era, an infant was expected to live until the age of 24, only marginally lower than in the 1300s in England (24.3 years). Additionally, the infant mortality rate in the first year of life was greater in Egypt than it was in England, so the average life expectancy after this critical first year was lower in England. The numbers from the 1300s are influenced by the Black Plague, which hit Europe in the middle of the century and had recurrent but smaller episodes until the end of the 1600s. In the middle of the 1700s, however, when the plague was history, the average life expectancy of an infant at birth was still a modest 33.7 years. Urbanization, which contributed negatively to population growth later in Europe's history, is also a part of the picture; during the Middle Ages, it had not progressed much.

A selection of point estimates help shed some light on development in the Middle Ages. Using the *Domesday Book* and *The Hundred Rolls*, a census conducted during 1279 and 1280, British economic historians compared the ability of English farmers to support themselves about a decade after William the Conqueror's invasion and then two hundred years later. Both inequality and poverty increased over these two centuries. At the time of the first tax assessment, the majority of agricultural households could earn a living by farming their own land. Two hundred years later, only 15 to 30 percent could do so, and they had to supplement their income as paid laborers in order to survive. This difference was caused by changes in the law during the thirteenth century, which made it possible to sell part of one's land to help make it through periods of bad harvest. Eventually, this short-sighted solution undermined the autonomy of small farmers. The mechanism behind the increase in inequality is thus the same as in Athens before the reforms of Solon.

Another glimpse into this time comes from medieval Paris in the form of tax rolls used under King Philip the Fair circa 1300. A Gini coefficient of 0.7 has been estimated—a high level of inequality. A number of estimates are also available for countries outside Western Europe. The score for Byzantium around the year 1000 was 0.41. Like the score for Ancient Rome, it might seem low but behind it lie quite varying distributions, which are revealed when they are assessed using other measures. In Byzantium, the wealthiest percentile of the population stood for 30 percent of the income, whereas in Rome that number was 16 percent.

Slavery was widespread in Europe during most of the Middle Ages, but it gradually lost its importance in the West. In Sweden, Magnus Eriksson introduced a ban on slavery in the mid-1300s, but it was limited to Christians, and there was nothing to stop people from keeping non-Christian slaves. Eastern Europe developed differently, and serfdom increased during the 1500s and 1600s. Taking a global view, the trans-oceanic slave trade began to develop in the 1400s.

## Modern Examples

With the dawn of the new era, opportunities opened up for new industries, international trade, and financial markets. The average income rose in Western Europe, while the distribution of income was affected in different ways. There are relatively detailed studies of England (later Great Britain) from the 1200s to the 1900s and of the Netherlands from the 1500s to the 1900s. In England, the more affluent classes usurped a growing share of society's wealth, at least until the mid-nineteenth century, when inequality leveled out. A similar pattern has been observed in the United States. From the end of the nineteenth century until the 1970s, inequality decreased in most industrialized countries, and then was back on the rise.

In Scandinavia, the Netherlands, Germany, and France,

development patterns differ in relation to the strength of the factors working for and against rising inequality. Important to development in the twentieth century was the state's growth and the development of social and fiscal policies, which in some countries would prove to have a strong impact on disposable household income.

Even though the richer OECD countries are similar in many respects, there are prevailing differences with regard to income distribution, as shown in Table 3.1 on the next page.

Because these countries are economically and socially similar, the main explanation for the differences in the distribution patterns lies in economic policies. For instance, income distribution can be influenced through tax and transfer systems. Nonetheless, the trend toward increasing disparity in income since 1970 is noticeable in most OECD countries; the differences have increased by 16 percent on average in the past two decades alone. In countries with relatively high ambitions for redistribution, such as Australia, Canada, Finland, and Sweden, more than half of the market-driven increase in income disparity has been offset by their tax and transfer systems, but in the rest, less than half of the difference has been offset.

Sweden does not deviate from the general pattern; equality rose from the late nineteenth century through to circa 1970, at which point the country saw an increase in inequality. Changes in Sweden's Gini index over the past decades can be seen in Diagram 3.1 on page 49.

An important aspect of the income distribution is the

| COUNTRY, YEAR | GINI COEFFICIENT |
|---|---|
| Denmark, 2000 | 0.225 |
| The Netherlands, 1999 | 0.231 |
| Finland, 2000 | 0.246 |
| Slovenia, 1999 | 0.249 |
| Norway, 2000 | 0.251 |
| Sweden, 2000 | 0.252 |
| Austria, 2000 | 0.257 |
| Luxembourg, 2000 | 0.260 |
| Germany, 2000 | 0.275 |
| France, 2000 | 0.278 |
| Belgium, 2000 | 0.279 |
| Switzerland, 2000 | 0.280 |
| Taiwan, 2000 | 0.296 |
| Ireland, 2000 | 0.313 |
| Japan, 1992 | 0.315 |
| Canada, 2000 | 0.315 |
| Australia, 2001 | 0.317 |
| Italy, 2000 | 0.334 |
| Greece, 2000 | 0.334 |
| Spain, 2000 | 0.336 |
| Great Britain, 1999 | 0.343 |
| Israel, 2001 | 0.346 |
| Portugal, 2000 | 0.363 |
| USA, 2000 | 0.368 |

Table 3.1. The Gini coefficients for a number of OECD countries around the year 2000. The countries are ordered according to increasing Gini coefficients. (Source: OECD)

relative importance of incomes from different sources, above all from labor and capital, which has been highlighted by French economist Thomas Piketty in his book, *Capital in the Twenty-First Century*. The facts presented in the book are the result of a collaborative effort of a large number of economists during many years, and the historical record has not been seriously questioned. What Piketty and his colleagues show is that the weight of capital in the economy increased till the last decades of the nineteenth century, whereupon it lost in importance during and between the world wars. After World War II, the importance of capital has grown steadily, even if the

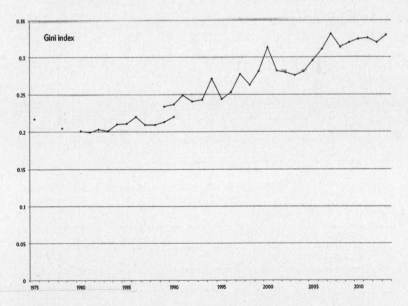

Diagram 3.1. Gini coefficient for disposable income in Sweden, 1975–2013. The break in the curve between 1989 and 1990 is a result of a change in the method of calculation. (Source: Statistics Sweden)

process looks somewhat different in the countries that have been studied. The share of capital income in total income has increased accordingly. What the debate has been about is the future development. Piketty claims that the importance of capital will continue to increase, whereas other participants in the debate highlight factors that work in the opposite direction.

Worldwide, the disparities are even greater. In the roughly 130 countries on which the World Bank has collected income distribution data, the Gini coefficient varies between 0.2 (Slovakia) and 0.74 (Namibia). There is a negative correlation between the GDP per capita and the Gini coefficient in this cross-section of countries. That is, the higher the level of development, the more equal the distribution—but it would be hasty to conclude that economic development leads to a more equal distribution. This connection is complex, and the relationship between growth and income distribution can go either way.

The global Gini index peaked in the 1980s and has sunk somewhat since. For the most recent period, the shift can be explained by the development in two countries: China and India. Over a longer time span—from the start of the 1800s to the late 1900s—statistics make it possible to break down global inequality into two parts: average variation within countries and the differences between countries themselves. It turns out that the former has been more or less constant during this entire period. And so, it is the increasing disparity between countries that explains the global rise in inequality.

# Theoretical and Factual Inequality

When you compare the Gini coefficient of various societies, it is important to keep in mind that the current level of development limits how wide the gap can grow between individuals' incomes or assets. In a hunter-gatherer society, where everyone is more or less living at the subsistence level, there simply is no room for inequality, because resources have to be shared equally to ensure that everyone will survive. It is only when there is a surplus that inequality between individuals can develop. The theoretically highest level of inequality occurs when the entire surplus is controlled by one person or a small group, while everyone else is living at the subsistence level, usually set at $400 in today's currency. The size of the ruling group is less important, as long as it is small. Economists Branko Milanović, Peter Lindert, and Jeffrey Williamson have used it to place a number of societies in relation to the theoretically highest level of inequality consistent with current levels of economic development—what they call the *inequality possibility frontier*. They have collected Gini coefficients from a wide range of societies over the past two millennia. For older societies, the household budget reports that provide the foundation for modern analyses are not available, but one can get surprisingly far with social tables that describe the most important strata, as well as occupational groups in a society, along with their relative positions on the income scale.

The results are summarized in Diagram 3.2 on the next page, which for simplicity's sake is drawn so that more-equal

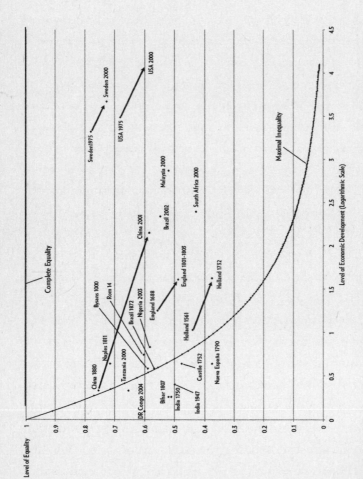

Diagram 3.2. The relationship between the level of economic development and equality. The horizontal axis shows the level of development measured by the average median income in relation to subsistence levels ($400 per year in today's currency), the vertical axis shows how equal the income distribution is (1 minus the Gini index). The curve in the lower part of the diagram is the limit of inequality—that is, the highest level of inequality possible in relation to the society's current level of development. (Source: Milanović et al. [2007] and OECD statistics)

societies appear closer to the top of the diagram. It shows how equal the distribution has been (the vertical axis) in the societies at various levels of development (the horizontal axis). The curve in the lower part of the diagram shows the theoretically calculated maximum inequality (the inequality possibility frontier). Certain societies, for example in the Democratic Republic of the Congo in 2004 and the Indian province of Bihar in 1807, have gone below this limit, meaning that the subsistence level in these societies is below the assumed $400 per year and that it is possible to further concentrate a society's resources. Alternatively, the poorest strata have access to resources that are not recorded.

It is interesting to see how economic development can change a society. Have a look at the following examples in the diagram: China in 1880 and 2001, England in 1688 and 1801–1803, and Holland in 1561 and 1732. The pattern is the same: inequality increases alongside economic development during the relevant periods. These are isolated examples, but enough to suggest a pattern.

Inequality increases in the present-day examples, but the distance to the inequality limit also increases. In other words, a transmission of economic power has occurred parallel to the increase in inequality. The diagram illustrates what was suggested earlier: when all, or almost all, of the population lives at the subsistence level, there is no room for inequality. It is economic development that makes way for inequality, as well as for a political opportunity to distribute the surplus in various ways. The relationship between actual inequality and the inequality limit—what Milanović and his colleagues call the *extraction ratio*—is a measure of how efficiently the ruling group extracts the surplus from the rest of the population. So, the increased distance to the inequality limit during times of rapid economic development shows how hard it is for the ruling elite to keep full control over the distribution of resources in periods like these.

## In Summary

Keeping in mind all the prudent reservations one might have when attempting to address the history of inequality in just a few pages, we can still try to capture its essence in a few stylized facts.

In primate societies, of which chimpanzees are among the most studied, there are indeed instances of inequality. The leaders have privileged access to food, enjoy sexual perks, and have above-average influence over collective decision-making. If there is an occasional surplus of food, they seek to and often gain control over the distribution of this surplus. In return, they are expected to resolve conflicts and ensure that the females and their young are given a reasonable share of the collective resources. On the other hand, there are clear limits to the leader's influence. Small groups are always stronger than a single alpha male, so he is always reliant on coalitions and therefore vulnerable to changes in the network. Because apes cannot store and accumulate resources, there are very clear limits to how large the differences between individuals can grow.

*Hunter-gatherer societies* are relatively equal, but there are still variances in this category. The same applies to *horticultural societies*, among which the variation is even greater. As with primates, these societies live to survive, so there is limited room for inequality. The opportunity to transmit resources between generations is also limited. Another important point is that these are small societies in which direct social control can be effective, and in which reciprocity as a mechanism for social control is easier to establish and maintain than in a larger society.

Inequality is greater in *pastoral societies* and increases even more when societies become *settled*. Settlements facilitate the accumulation of resources, which can then be exploited by leaders in order to cultivate and assert differences in status, for example through the size of their homes, control over supplies, and distribution of surplus. Here, transmission between generations is more important than in hunter-gatherer societies, and it aids the accumulation of prosperity in certain families.

These tendencies intensify as the society becomes *agricultural*. The division of labor develops. A crucial step occurs when the ruling class has sufficient resources to employ armed forces, thereby securing a monopoly on organized violence.

In summary: when we take a long historical view, we see a clear tendency toward rising inequality. Inequality moves toward the level that the current stage of development allows—the inequality possibility frontier. If a social equilibrium characterized by equality is upset and certain individuals or groups get the upper hand in the fight for power, there is no natural force that can return a society to its previous equilibrium.

Sudden changes in the environment, such as technical progress or other discoveries, can open up new channels to power and lead to spreading prosperity; the modernization of Europe and the rise of the bourgeoisie is perhaps the most important example of this tendency. But even under these circumstances, such opportunities are often most skillfully exploited by those previously in power, and so the general power structure may emerge relatively intact from such periods of change.

The notable exception to the general pattern of rising inequality, which is practically unique in size and scope, is the leveling-out of wealth in the twentieth century following unionization, democratization, and the growth of the welfare state.

When egalitarian societies are described in the literature, the limits of inequality set by their environs are rarely discussed. There is no reason to believe that people in hunter-gatherer cultures have a different constitution or capacity to exert moral pressure that would curb the power of a ruling class. These societies are egalitarian quite simply because there is very little room for inequality when a society is close to the subsistence level. In societies with a larger surplus of goods, what restricts the power imbalance between the affluent and the impoverished is the former's interest in keeping the latter alive and reasonably fit for work. Inequality will rise until it hits this limit, it seems. And this is the relationship that needs to be explained.

# 4

## THE END OF THE TALE

If two identical players are bargaining over a resource,
they will divide it evenly. But what happens if one player
has more resources at the start?

Sweet little child, the story ends here:
the young royals arrived in their kingdom
and were greeted with pomp and cheer.
As for you, the time for slumber has come.

What happened next? Well, there's not much to say,
once their dangerous quest was finally done,
things happened that happen here every day
to you and me and everyone.

The years passed and the princess grew old and fat
the prince too grew old but bony,
she got migraines and had family spats,
he waged war and was gouty.

*But never you mind, now's not the time for worry,*
*Nestle in and lay your head down,*
*and dream you are that very prince,*
*who carried the princess to safer ground.*

*And once your dreams have taken you that far,*
*the sun will have found you in bed,*
*Then quick, you'll rise quick and put your clothes on,*
*for tomorrow there's hay to be shred.*

—SIGFRID LINDSTRÖM, "The End of the Tale"

Social contract theorists—Lucretius to Marsilius of Padua, Hobbes and Locke to modern philosophers like Rawls and Nozick—have all tried to find the perfect contract, the one that would righteously lead the hypothetical people of a nationless society from one generation to the next in their march through history. Their solutions have varied over the centuries, but the blueprint has remained the same. A political theory with this goal must take into account the social mechanisms that will steer development after contract negotiations are done. To think only as far as the moment when the contract is signed is like wrapping up the story once the prince saves the princess from the dragon and they live happily ever after. That is not the end of the tale; it is only the beginning.

How should we imagine a group of people gathering together in some way to sign a social contract? There has been no such event in history. The situation that comes closest to this ideal occurs when new countries are faced with the task of drafting a constitution following a war of independence, for example. But even in these relatively open situations, the authors of the constitution are beholden to a prehistory and a social structure that must be kept in mind for the constitutional project to succeed. And the shape of the contract will most likely be influenced by differences in wealth and social status.

As a thought experiment, try to picture this scenario. You would have to assume that the individuals are identical in the ways that can influence how the social contract takes shape. Individual differences should not be allowed to come to the fore, as when moral norms are discussed. This does not mean that there will not be any significant differences. Once the contract is signed, it will emerge that some people prefer to live in populated areas and engage in commerce, while others prefer to devote themselves to agriculture. Certain people will be entrepreneurial and prone to taking risks, and others more careful. It is to be expected that some people will try to lead a parasitic existence, and the contract must also take this eventuality into account.

Another primary assumption should be that everyone enters the game with the same basic conditions—material, intellectual, and so on—but that they might manage their assets in different ways. How life will then unfold cannot be predicted with much precision. There will be both positive and negative surprises—unexpected discoveries, natural disasters, and so on. If you believe that the starting point of the game should reflect the conditions for a majority of humanity for the majority of history, then their living conditions will be close to the subsistence level.

One thing is certain: the resulting society will be defined by the division of labor and collective effort, and thus negotiations over how the fruits of this labor should be distributed. Some people hunt, others gather. Among those who hunt, some scare up the prey, others catch it. People have to trade the fruits of their labor, and this means that the terms of those trades should be set—that bargaining will take place, in the open or implicitly. And so, how these negotiations turn out is crucial to the continued development of society.

## The Elementary Negotiation

The overview in Chapter 2 showed that bargaining can be considered an elementary building block of social relations. In the previous chapter, we saw that inequality generally tends to increase over time. This is a tendency, not a natural law; changes in the players' surroundings impact their bargaining power and development fluctuates accordingly. Let us identify the main tendency and see if it can be linked with the act of bargaining in society. Is there a mechanism inherent in bargaining itself that leads to imbalances? Can negotiation be described in general enough terms so as to elucidate a typical transaction without becoming meaningless?

The simplest instance of bargaining takes place between

two players who have something that needs to be shared—spoils of the hunt, this year's harvest, a loaf of bread, etc. The two players can be individuals—Robinson Crusoe and Friday in the smallest of all imaginable societies—but it is more natural to think in terms of groups that act in concert—landowners versus leaseholders, master of the house versus servants, capitalist versus employees—as long as the individuals within each group largely share the same interests.

This is not about a single instance of negotiation, but a long-term relationship where meetings happen more or less regularly, perhaps once a year, to determine the distribution. Between those meetings, what is gained through bargaining is consumed. For the description to be representative, keep in mind that for the majority of history, the majority of people have lived close to the subsistence level. Consequently, the time frame in question is short; it is necessary to focus on the immediate future so as to be able to survive until the next harvest or paycheck. Therefore, having a long-standing relationship with the other player will not have a significant impact on the dealings.

For the problem to be meaningful, it must be assumed that each player has a buffer; otherwise it would spell certain death if a player does not receive the share needed to survive.

Here we have the most simplified stylized bargaining scenario possible: two parties in a subsistence economy, bargaining at regular intervals, each with a buffer that allows them to survive temporary fluctuations in the outcome. At first, the process is symmetrical because both individuals begin with the same conditions. But what will happen to this relationship in the long run?

## Bargaining According to Nash

In the simplest of all bargaining scenarios, there are two individuals who have something that needs to be shared. But how? If you have no further information about the situation, most people would probably suggest that it be divided equally. But what happens when you do have more information?

Some will want to hear the backstory. How was the bread made? Who tilled the land, who reaped, who sowed? Who kneaded the dough and kept an eye on the bread while it was baking? Others will go by need. Who is the hungriest? Who has the most mouths to feed? Who has the best chances of doing more work? These suggestions are based on externally imposed norms. A more distanced approach is to leave the decision up to those involved; whatever they agree on is a legitimate solution.

Even if you choose the latter approach, you probably have an idea of what would constitute a reasonable solution. For instance, both players must reach an agreement without threatening or using violence. This condition will likely be met if it is assumed that there will be a continuation—new hunting business, continued work in agriculture—at least for the foreseeable future. Otherwise there will not be another hunting expedition. One basic requirement is that both players get something out of the process. Another is that everything be apportioned; there is no reason to leave anything on the table.

A demand for symmetry is also natural. If the conditions are symmetrical, the solution should be, too.

A more technical question: can the conversation be restricted to realistic-seeming solutions? It is not uncommon to issue threats when bargaining, but the threats must be realistic to be believable. So it is reasonable to imagine that the solution would stay the same if the analysis were to be limited to options that both players deem realistic.

Following his groundbreaking work in the early 1950s, the mathematician John Nash became one of modern game and bargaining theory's leading figures. Sadly, his career was cut short by illness. Nash showed that the above demands, together with the purely mathematical-technical condition that the solution be independent of the scale used to measure the players' utility, leads to a unique solution that can be expressed in mathematical terms.

In order to describe the solution, you need the term *utility function*, one of the most important analytical tools in economics. The simplest way of explaining a utility function is to say that it describes how a person experiences the consumption of something—goods or services—and how the experience changes in relation to the amount consumed. What would this function look like? Diagram 4.1 on the next page gives an example of this.

First, utility should grow in pace with supply: "more is better." Meanwhile, we are under the well-founded impres-

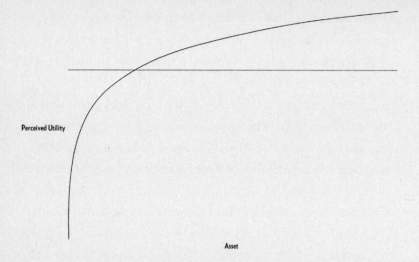

Diagram 4.1. A typical utility function curve. Utility increases in line with the assets—the curve points upward—but utility grows more slowly the larger the asset—the curve bends downward.

sion that utility grows more slowly the larger the supply; there is a saturation effect. The relationship between the intensity that people feel and the magnitude of physical stimulus was investigated in the 1800s by the German psychologists Ernst Heinrich Weber and Gustav Theodor Fechner, and a special mathematical expression—the Weber-Fechner law—that summarizes their findings. There is empirical evidence for the law's application to simpler stimuli, like sound and vision; whether or not it is a valid description of how we experience the world is open to discussion.

Nash's solution to the bargaining problem presupposes that there is a utility function for both Players 1 and 2, $u_1$ and $u_2$ respectively. The solution can be illustrated geometrically, as in the diagram above. The outcome for both players is measured along the axes. The starting point for negotiations is always zero (the origin), where the axes intersect. In the worst case—no agreement—the players get nothing and stay at zero. The solution should be sought within the curve that describes the possible outcomes for both players, a curve that is determined in part by how both players experience the utility of various levels of consumption, and in part by how much is up for negotiation. The solution will in fact be found on this curve. Nash showed that the unique solution is given by the point that maximizes the surface area of the rectangle with the sides $u_1$ and $u_2$ in Diagram 4.2 on the next page.

In the decades since Nash presented his work, other researchers have explored different sets of assumptions. Though alternatives have been presented, Nash's solution remains the most credible and widely accepted. Interestingly, the same conclusion can be reached using other methods. It could also be imagined as a series of alternating bids, as in the classical bidding model, where the players still share an interest in reaching a solution. Under general conditions, this approach will lead to the same solution, when the bargaining intervals shrink toward zero. This is one of the model's strengths, in that it yields an interesting stylized description of an actual event, and not just as the result of a mathematical-technical deduction with abstractly defined demands on the solution.

This last point is important. Whereas other approaches to describing and analyzing the problem often take a valuation as their starting point—e.g., equality is ideal—Nash's analysis is

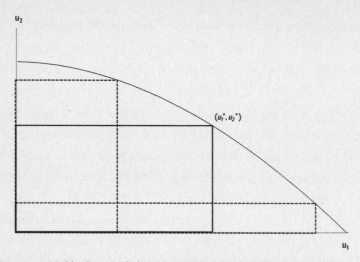

Diagram 4.2. Nash's solution to the bargaining problem. The available options are the ones found in-side the curve. The outcomes for both players, $u_1{}^*$ and $u_2{}^*$ respectively, are given by the point that maximizes the surface area of the rectangle with the sides $u_1$ and $u_2$ in the diagram. The solid rectangle represents the optimum solution, and the dotted rectangles have smaller surface areas and thus represent inferior options.

descriptive. It stems from intellectual—rather than ethical—demands.

So what does Nash's solution look like in practice? If two identical players are bargaining over a resource, they will divide it evenly. But what happens if one player has more assets from the start?

Most people can probably guess that a player who has more resources at the beginning of the bargaining process has a good chance of getting a larger piece of the pie. That player is better equipped to wait, to take risks—the biggest risk being that nothing will come of bargaining and both players will walk away empty-handed. It is natural to assume that the advantages the player has at the start of bargaining will be reflected in the payoff. And this assumption can be proven. It becomes necessary to add the condition that the likelihood of taking risks increases as assets increase—this is an assumption backed by experiential evidence, not a given. With this condition included, the intuitive assumption is confirmed: whoever has more resources when the bargaining begins will also get a better payoff.

## The Long-term Dynamic of the Bargaining Game

In order to turn Nash's static bargaining problem into a dynamic one, the additional conditions described above must be included. We begin with two players who have produced something together and are to negotiate the payoff. They live close to the subsistence level. In other words, supply during a certain time period—a month, year, or whatever seems relevant—is equal to the demand. Nash's solution to the static problem provides us with the starting point for bargaining in each time period. Each player has a buffer, which allows them to temporarily weather periods where the payoff of the bargaining game does not entirely meet the demands of consumption. In the simplest formulation, we can assume that each player continues to consume the same amount, however large the buffer.

If the starting point for dynamic bargaining is completely

symmetrical, the solution will be, too. Nash's bargaining solution gives each player an equal amount in each time period, they consume equal amounts, and they arrive at the next round of bargaining with the same prerequisites. Hence, the solution will be equal for all periods thereafter.

Now assume that the starting point is disrupted, so that one of the players begins bargaining with a slightly stronger position than the other. Nash's basic solution would then give that player a slightly larger share of the collective production. If the player who now has received more than half consumes the same amount as before, then the surplus will be added to that player's buffer, while the other party will be forced to use his part of the buffer to cover his needs of consumption. The player who was better off at the start of bargaining will return to the next round of negotiations in an even stronger position. And he can then expect an even larger payoff, and so on. The long-term effect is easy to see; the assets of one player will grow at an ever-increasing rate, while those of the other will be depleted just as quickly. This is an example of what is technically called *positive feedback*, whereby a certain change is intensified by the system's dynamics and leads to instability. It might look like the Diagram 4.3, where one player starts with 1 percent greater assets than the other, i.e., 1.01 units, and the other player starts with a buffer of 1 unit. After 70 or 80 periods, the weaker player's assets are depleted.

The mechanism applies if the players are operating within a short time-span; that is, they are bargaining over the surplus of one period at a time. This is a reasonable assumption if the

players are living at or close to the subsistence level—the status quo for most of humanity for most of history.

Now, if we return to our abstract individuals who are
about to sign a social contract with each other, it is clear that
this mechanism is relevant to the drafting of the contract. Even
if they are identical—physically and intellectually, creatively,
energetically, and in any other way that can impact the outcome—their lives will at some point diverge. There will always
be minor disruptions in our surroundings that will affect the
result through no fault of anyone. Everyone might be given an
equally large plot of land, but one party's plot might be more
fertile. Another might lose part of her herd to a contagious

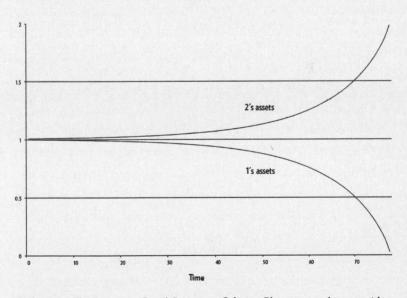

Diagram 4.3. The Bargaining Game's Long-term Solution. Player 2 starts the game with 1
percent greater assets than Player 1, who has a buffer that will see him through an entire
period. After 70 or 80 periods, Player 1's assets are depleted.

disease. A third could lose his house after it is struck by lightning and burns to the ground. Such natural and unpredictable events are part of life.

What the reasoning above shows is that these minor differences will be intensified by the very dynamics of the bargaining game, resulting in rising inequality. There is no natural equilibrium at which the process would stop of its own accord. The only thing that, in practice, will limit the stronger player's resources is an interest in keeping the other player alive so work can continue.

There is indeed room for refinement in this highly simplified example. It was assumed that both players consume equal amounts, even if one gets a larger payoff and so has the opportunity to consume more. In reality, one would expect the person who has more to consume more, but not so much as to threaten her position in anticipation of the next round of negotiations. This slows the process down, but it does not lead to a qualitatively different outcome.

This analysis is limited to two players. Nash's results can in some cases be generalized to include three or more players, but there is no general theory for coalitions that could lay the groundwork for an analysis of the problem at large. At the same time, it is important to underscore that the analysis holds for situations in which the two players are natural coalitions rather than individuals.

When the players are groups of individuals rather than individuals, the situation becomes more complicated. First it must be noted that these situations have historically tended to be asymmetrical as far as the number of individuals in each group. There have always been fewer landowners than there have been farmworkers, fewer owners of capital than employees, etc. And organizational problems are always greater for larger groups. This even extends to a well-organized large group, which might appear strong in a showdown. However, the amount of risk the group is willing to take when negotiating is determined at the fringes by individuals, and if its members are living close to the subsistence level, the group itself becomes vulnerable. Large groups of individuals with limited resources have a double handicap. If anything, the conclusion is exacerbated. In this less commonly cited passage from *The Wealth of Nations*, Adam Smith had already made note of the unequal starting points in Great Britain in the late 1700s:

> What are the common wages of labour depends every where upon the contract usually made between those two parties, whose interests are by no means the same. [. . .]
>
> It is not, however, difficult to foresee which of the two parties must, upon all ordinary occasions, have the advantage in the dispute, and force the other into a compliance with their terms. The masters, being fewer in number, can combine much more easily: and the law, besides, authorises, or at least does not prohibit, their combinations, while it prohibits those of

the workmen. We have no acts of parliament against combining to lower the price of work; but many against combining to raise it. In all such disputes, the masters can hold out much longer. A landlord, a farmer, a master manufacturer, or merchant, though they did not employ a single workman, could generally live a year or two upon the stocks which they have already acquired. Many workmen could not subsist a week, few could subsist a month, and scarce any a year without employment. In the long-run, the workman may be as necessary to his master as his master is to him; but the necessity is not so immediate.

So far, the analysis has been limited to interaction between two parties, but it can be generalized to a modern market economy, as shown by Ricardo and Robert Fernholz. Imagine a society inhabited by individuals that are identical with respect to capabilities and efforts. They interact over a financial market where they place the surplus that is not consumed. The yield is subject to chance fluctuations. Even if all individuals have equal assets at the outset, such fluctuations will lead to differences in assets which will affect their behavior in the financial market. If we assume, as experience tells us, that more assets imply that the owner can afford to take somewhat higher risks, those who are lucky in the first round will be rewarded by a higher yield in the second round, because higher risk corres-

ponds to higher yield. The self-reinforcing mechanism that we
have seen in a two-person interaction is also active here. Small
differences in assets will be magnified, concentration will increase with time, and in the limit, all assets will be owned by
one single individual. Chance is the only driving force here;
the outcome has nothing to do with differences in capabilities
or effort, because all individuals are identical in these respects.

How surprised you are by this conclusion depends on
your expectations. It is unsurprising that a person who arrives
at a negotiation in a stronger position will get a larger payoff
at the end; we experience this more or less daily in our everyday lives, on the job market, or in politics. But the conclusion
that a symmetrical starting point, where both players have the
same essential resources, will in the long run lead to distinctly
asymmetrical results is perhaps more surprising. Nash's own
conclusion for each round of negotiations is, on the contrary,
built on the assumption that symmetrical starting points lead
to symmetrical conclusions. In this sense, the conclusion is
less expected.

## Model and Reality

Let us go back to the reality that was summarized in Chapter 3.
As history has shown, the self-reinforcing mechanism driving
the development of the bargaining process is consistent with
the general tendency toward rising inequality. This is not an
uninterrupted development, but as a stylized fact on a highly

abstract level, it summarizes the general tendency rather well. The big exception is the decrease in inequality from the late 1800s to the 1970s. This deviation from the general pattern is not a mystery and can be explained by the creation of unions and the introduction of universal suffrage. The unions were a fairly equal match for the owners of capital, which changed the conditions during pay negotiations. Universal suffrage gave the people's majority the chance to develop a public sector that offered education, healthcare, social security, and other basic universal services, regardless of social background or financial resources. The mostly tax-financed expansion of the public sector after the Second World War provided a mechanism that could balance out the bargaining game's natural tendency toward inequality.

The creation of trade unions and the fight for universal suffrage as such are problematic for individual theories of rationality, because what a single union member or suffragette gains from their engagement rarely matches the amount of work they put in, but that is more a problem for rational-actor theorists than it is for the bargaining game.

The reason for the return of the tendency toward rising inequality in the 1970s—simply put—relates to globalization. The evolution of transport and communication networks led to the rapid integration of national and regional markets with the global market. The systems that were developed in the 1900s to level out the distribution of disposable income through taxation and transfer payments are primarily national, and more than anything else it has done, globalization has increased the room for maneuver of capital. Capital can be moved with a phone call or a keystroke, but the process of mobilizing unions and homogenizing laws across national borders and between continents is a time-consuming and complicated process.

It is not as though the political right presented fresh, strong arguments against the equal distribution of society's resources during the later decades of the twentieth century. Rising inequality from the 1970s forward was the result of other technological and economic changes, and the turning of the ideological tide was a reflection of these changes, not their origin.

## The Bridge Between *Is* and *Ought*

And so we see that negotiations—essential to human societies on all levels—are fundamentally unstable. There is no stable equilibrium with a reasonable equitable distribution of society's resources. This is a fact. But are facts relevant to an ideological discussion? David Hume established that facts are qualitatively different to values; collections of facts cannot proffer recommendations, neither can an *ought to* be drawn from an *is*. Modern research into logic has confirmed this conclusion; a *bridge principle* is needed to connect facts with recommendations.

What Hume's observation does not account for is that some facts lend themselves more to recommendations than do others. If a group of people visiting a house is informed that the house was built in 1752, this does not suggest a course of action. If someone rushes into the room and shouts, "The house is on fire!," this is still a fact. In contrast to the previous assertion, a normative conclusion will follow—the visitors should get out of the house as quickly as possible. The implicit assumption that makes it possible to draw a conclusion on how to act—the bridge principle—is that the visitors want to survive the day, something that can be taken as a given. This is how the relationship between the previous conclusions and ideologies are meant to be interpreted. They make some ideological positions easier to take than others.

# 5

## THE ART OF FLYING

*Feedback from the current state of society is needed
to keep each social development in check.*

Negotiation—central to every human society, in all spheres
and on every level—suffers from an inherent instability. Differences in power that correspond to differences in the strength
of bargaining positions tend to intensify as a result of the dynamics inherent to the negotiation process. It is a simple fact
that cannot be bypassed in either political philosophy or practical politics. Unstable systems are problematic, but in most
cases they can be managed. Technically speaking, instability
can even be built into the design, and practical experiences of
stabilizing unstable mechanical systems do have a certain relevance to political-philosophical discussions.

On December 17, 1903, in a field in Kitty Hawk, North Caro-
lina, the Wright brothers—Wilbur and Orville—became the

first people in history to leave the ground and pilot an independent, heavier-than-air flying machine. Around lunch time, after they each took a few short flights, Wilbur managed to keep the machine in the air for a distance of 250 meters. Orville's words marked this modest beginning:

> It was nevertheless the first time in the history
> of the world in which a machine carrying a man
> had raised itself by its own power into the air
> in full flight, had sailed forward without reduc-
> tion of speed, and had finally landed at a point
> as high as that from which it had started.

This event had enormous implications for fields as wide-ranging as security policy, international trade, and the spread of contagious diseases. There are many insights to be gathered about knowledge-building and design principles from the story of how we learned to fly.

The Wright brothers were not alone in their ambitions. In the United States and in other countries, many groups were trying to be the first to get a heavier-than-air machine into the sky. The main competitor in the United States was a group led by Samuel Pierpont Langley, an influential secretary of the Smithsonian Institution in Washington, D.C. Langley's group nearly succeeded in getting an unmanned plane into the air in May 1896 and convinced the federal government to put up funds for the project—starting with the then-considerable sum of $25,000. After many difficulties and failures, two test flights were made on October 7 and December 8, 1903. Both attempts were disastrous; each time the Aerodrome, as it was called, plunged into the Potomac River as soon as it left the launch pad. Ten days after this attempt, the Wright brothers' flying machine was in the air.

Why did the Wright brothers succeed and Langley's group meet with disaster? Clearly, it had nothing to do with their resources. The federal project would end up costing around $70,000 before it was terminated. Wilbur Wright estimated their expenses to have been less than $1,000. Ample material resources are no guarantee for success.

For the duration of the project, Langley was obsessed with developing an efficient motor, where performance was measured by the amount of horsepower per kilogram of the engine's weight. His extremely competent head engineer, Charles Manly, ended up installing a motor that could deliver more than 50 horsepower but weighed under 90 kilograms. With less than 2 kilograms per horsepower, it was by far the most advanced motor in use as part of the mission to develop a flying machine at the time, and it was four times as efficient as the Wright brothers'.

Though Langley's motor was a brilliant feat of engineering, the plane's design left something to be desired. But Langley stuck to his 1896 design, which resembled a monstrous dragonfly. Its bowed wings were inspired by bird's wings but had not been developed using systematic trials. Langley was sure the machine would fly if only he had a good enough motor.

The Wright brothers approached the problem from a com-

The Wright brothers at Kitty Hawk, December 17, 1903. (Photograph by John T. Daniels. Library of Congress, Washington, D.C.)

pletely different angle. They started by building kites and learned about aerodynamics through trial and error. The knowledge they were building on came primarily from Otto Lilienthal, who had experimented with hang-gliders and died in an accident during a trial run in 1896. Lilienthal in turn was building on aerodynamic research conducted by the eighteenth-century British engineer John Smeaton. The Wright brothers became increasingly dissatisfied with Lilienthal's data, so they conducted small-scale experiments on optimum wing shape in their own workshop. In numerous experiments, they learned how to adjust the altitude and to turn. Only when they believed they were done with the aerodynamic design did they begin to think about the motor. They contacted a few manufacturers with their performance and weight specifications, which were far more modest than Langley's. Dissatisfied with the responses, they decided to build their own motor out of parts from the local forge. It was installed, and then they had liftoff.

The first lesson from Kitty Hawk is that success hinges on understanding the system you want to influence: how it behaves, its dynamics and peculiarities. Langley was right in thinking that there was a minimum performance requirement on the motor for the plane to be able to achieve liftoff, but he was wrong in thinking that this was the most significant constraint in aircraft design. The Wright brothers realized that the fundamental problem was one of aerodynamics and made solving it their priority. Only when they had developed a near-perfect maneuverable kite did they begin to tackle the motor.

There are other, more specific lessons to be drawn about the design principles themselves. Most of the Wrights' predecessors who constructed gliders and airplanes had worked with models that were stable as far as tipping was concerned—that is, the angle between the plane's longitudinal axis and the horizontal plane. After minor disturbances of the tipping angle, a stable plane returns to the desired angle. The Wright brothers allowed their airplane to be unstable, which afforded them the maneuverability needed to fly. But this design came with a price: the pilot was under the constant stress of having to adjust the elevator to keep the plane at a steady altitude. Wilbur Wright noted the constant need to practice:

> Skill comes by the constant repetition of famil-
> iar feats rather than by a few overbold attempts
> at feats for which the performer is yet poorly
> prepared [. . .] A thousand glides is equivalent
> to about four hours of steady practice, far too
> little to give anyone a complete mastery of the
> art of flying.

To relieve the pilot of this tiring task, they needed to develop an autopilot, which would take care of the continual adjustments needed to keep the plane horizontal and at a constant height. The person who made this contribution was Elmer Sperry, then one of America's most successful engineers with many navigational inventions under his belt. Not ten years after Kitty Hawk, he had developed an autopilot, which was presented in Paris. With Sperry's autopilot in place, the pilot's job was limited to setting the course, altitude, and speed, after which a servo and an actuator took over.

Autopilots operate on the basis of measurements of angles, velocity, and other key variables. It is the key principle in *feedback*: constant measurement of at least a few of the variables that describe a system's status is essential to successful regulation. This also applies when the system that is being regulated is stable. For example, any attempt to steer a ship to its final destination by setting the course at the point of departure and hoping that it will hit its mark using only that information—what engineers call *feedforward*—will fail. The vessel will gradually veer off course because of unpredictable disruptions along the way.

When the controlled system is unstable, it is likely that such attempts will end in disaster. With a constant elevator setting, the Wright brothers' airplane will either dive toward the ground or climb into the air—both actions would eventually result in a crash. Taking constant measurements and getting feedback from the tipping angle are key to a successful flight.

## Creating Stability in an Uncertain World

Though the art of flying differs from both political philosophy and practical politics, the experiences at Kitty Hawk are still relevant. Knowing the system you wish to influence is just as important in all three arenas. The social sciences are lagging far behind physics when it comes to theoretical rigor and validity, but physics today has advanced far beyond where it was when the Wright brothers were working on their flight project. The brothers saw the necessity in seeking out the available theories and data and making the best of their material. Within practical politics and political philosophy, the situation is different. Classical philosophers such as Hobbes and Locke did not have the social sciences at their disposal and relied on their common sense, peppered with fragments of stories from abroad. Social scientists have evolved, but philosophy and praxis remain relatively unaltered, by and large proceeding in their pre-scientific state. Keynes once noted that "Practical men, who believe themselves to be quite exempt from any intellectual influences, are usually slaves of some defunct economist," and many a political philosopher takes after them in this respect.

Political praxis has evolved, in economic arenas most of all, but the focus that economists have placed on the market has led to a serious imbalance in the relationship between social sciences and policy making. Even more than political philosophy, politics suffers from what psychologists call *selective perception*: decision-makers tend to seek out research that supports (or that they believe supports) their current positions.

Instability can arise spontaneously or, as with Wright brothers' airplane, by design. In their case, the aim was to create a maneuverable machine. Whatever its origin, instability must be managed, and the techniques for doing so are now well established. The primary tool is feedback: a response that compensates for the system's own movement away from the desired equilibrium. The response must of course work against the system; the feedback must be *negative*. Moreover, it must be based on readings of the current status in the system. As in the mechanical examples, it is impossible to build stabilization into a program that uses advance calculations and does not continuously monitor the system's status.

We are approaching territory relevant to both moral and political philosophy and that relates indirectly to practical politics. What moral statements are supposed to be about has long been debated in philosophy. Should they say something about the state of the world, or about the events that lead to us to that state? The value of an action can be measured as such or by its consequences. In his book *Anarchy, State, and Utopia*, Robert Nozick makes a similar distinction between historical and end-result theories in political philosophy.

Taking an evolutionary view can yield a quite simple answer to this question. Norms are derived from problematic situations so as to make certain socially desirable actions more likely to occur than if the norm did not exist. A behavior is encouraged socially if it is highly likely to lead to desirable results. If the opposite is true, it is forbidden. The norm of telling the truth is needed to counteract the temptation to lie when it suits you; language would lose its value as a means of communication if people could not trust what was being said. Even if one can engineer a situation in which it would be morally correct to lie, the truth-norm will mostly yield better results. An action or policy can thus only be held up as a moral ideal on the basis of an evaluation of the social state to which it generally leads. Hence, rule- or principle-based moral systems are just as dependent on social outcomes as systems which are based on consequences, even if the dependency is more indirect than direct.

Moral norms and other codes of conduct are needed to free the individual from the unreasonable burden of predicting and evaluating the consequences of everyday actions. However, rules imply risks. Every valuation of a code of conduct is based on a limited number of examples, and so the valuation is always provisional. Even if norms are based on extensive experience, they are only templates; as in the example about truth-telling above, they might sometimes lead to the wrong result.

The parallels with Nozick's end-result and historical theories within political thought are clear. Codes and institutions are short-cuts that help us differentiate between desirable and undesirable decisions and measures. Because every political-philosophical ideology and every constitutional discussion is far from perfect, we must follow social developments and relate them back to fundamental ideals. Trying to base a political-philosophical ideal or constitution on an analysis conducted in advance is analogous to guiding a mechanical system using only feedforward: it is doomed to fail. Nozick's argument for historical principles and rule-based management lacks this crucial insight. The brushy terrain of political philosophy yields few pure errors, but this is an exception to the rule.

Let us illustrate the impossibility of formulating rule-based agreements in advance with two prime examples of failed social contracts. They will also help explain the terrible living conditions of Europe's population in the Middle Ages. First, the nobility was offered tax exemptions in exchange for military protection against outside enemies. Though attractive in its simplicity, the decision was not preceded by a thorough investigation. Decisions like this one were made at various points in time in Europe, but the setup was always the same. The contract paved the way for an unstemmed accumulation of wealth among a select few because none of the assets that the nobility acquired were redistributed in society. The monopoly on legitimate violence that the contract essentially handed to the nobility could of course be used against those who questioned whether or not the nobility was fulfilling its commitments, and indeed it was used thus.

In our second example, the church had a similar role. As part of the social contract established rather early in its history, priests had the right to tithes in exchange for keeping in touch with the divine realm and for engaging in some social-welfare activities. The tithe, Judaic in origin, was not immediately accepted by the Christian church. Paying 10 percent tax might seem reasonable, but again there had been no close investigation into whether perhaps 8 or 12 percent would have been better. Whether or not the tax rate was reasonable in relation to the services provided was not up for discussion by the time the church had established itself as an earthly power with far-reaching political ambitions and was using its resources to exert large-scale violence against its critics, at times as part of a shaky alliance with the nobility.

These are two historically significant examples of the impossibility of drafting rules that, in the absence of corrective mechanisms, do not lead to unforeseen and undesirable consequences. Feedback from the current state of society is needed to keep each social development within reasonable bounds.

As part of the political discussion, it is important to remember that a policy or control mechanism designed to keep the system within range of a desirable social state will never be perfect. The system is always vulnerable to disruption from various sources, and design imperfections make it impossible to do away with these disruptions entirely. A mechanism that has been developed to manage certain disruptions does not activate until the disruptions become apparent. In the same way, distribution policies can be created to reduce the effects of the inequality that arise from the instability of the negotiation process, but policies cannot eliminate these effects entirely, nor should they aim to.

# 6

## BACK TO THE SOCIAL CONTRACT

*Those who do not accept a moral or political*
*system based on religion, myth, or the status quo have*
*no alternative but the rational approach.*

Social contract theories have been central to political philos-ophy for more than two millennia, and they have had their share of critics. Hume states in an essay from 1742 titled "Of the Original Contract":

> The other party, by founding government alto-gether on the consent of the PEOPLE, suppose that there is a kind of *original contract*, by which the subjects have tacitly reserved the power of resisting their sovereign, whenever they find themselves aggrieved by that authority, with which they have, for certain purposes, volun-tarily entrusted him. [. . .] But the contract, on

which government is founded, is said to be the
*original contract*; and consequently may be supposed too old to fall under the knowledge of the
present generation. If the agreement, by which
savage men first associated and conjoined their
force, be here meant, this is acknowledged to
be real; but being so ancient, and being obliter-
ated by a thousand changes of government and
princes, it cannot now be supposed to retain
any authority.

For Hume, the social contract is a fiction. But even if it is, it is
clearly a fiction with power. An ideological reflex most likely
underlies Hume's and other conservative thinkers' critiques.
Prior to signing the contract, it is assumed that all people are
equal, at least insofar as it relates to the signing of the contract
itself. Everyone is equipped with a basic intellectual and moral
capacity, and everyone has the same right to reject the contract
if it does not meet reasonable demands. This fundamental
egalitarian starting point might seem objectionable to people
who believe that some groups have been naturally appointed
to govern a society, regardless of the merits on which those
privileges are founded.

Modern versions built on game or bargaining theory can
indeed be criticized on methodological grounds, too. Some
think it pathetic to use highly simplified models to tackle a
problem as complicated as a social contract. On the other
hand, the contract's complexity can be used as an argument in

favor of formal models, which at least guarantee a certain de-gree of internal consistency. The alternative—to conduct the discussion using language unsupported by a formal model—comes with its own risks.

## Classical and Medieval Thought

When the historical scene changed during the Hellenistic Period, an alternative to Plato's ideas about a ruling elite was needed. Aristotle expanded the political space and included the upper middle class. In the long term, the alternatives de-veloped by the Epicureans, Cynics, and Stoics were of greater importance. For them the *individual*—independent of nation, class, or religion—was the starting point for the political and philosophical discussion. The Stoic Chrysippus went so far as the include slaves by viewing them as hirelings for life. It is from this era that we have the term *oikoumene*, a global fellow-ship called humanity, as well as an expansive theory on funda-mental rights and obligations that can be defined and on some abstract level are the same for everyone.

However, the notion of natural law—the idea that humans have inalienable rights—is older. In Sophocles' *Antigone*, the protagonist defends a right conveyed by an authority higher than King Creon himself:

> *Nor did I deem that thou, a mortal man,*
> *Could'st by a breath annul and override*

*The immutable unwritten laws of Heaven.*
*They were not born today nor yesterday;*
*They die not; and none knoweth whence they sprang.*

The most famous Epicurean source text, Lucretius' *De rerum natura* (*On the Nature of Things*), includes many of modern contract theory's building blocks: the importance of natural impulses, the social contract as a solution to the problem of interpersonal conflict, and even an early version of an evolutionary theory for social development. There is also a Stoic version of natural law.

The Epicurean contract is symbolically undersigned by a group of individuals who relinquish a number of their natural rights in order to create the necessary conditions for peaceful coexistence. The supreme power to whom one cedes freedom of action is absent, and a divine authority does not even enter into the conversation. Medieval thinkers quite naturally put their discussion into a religious framework. Toward the end of the 1000s, Manegold of Lautenbach formulated a theory of political legitimacy. Manegold's goal was to articulate the difference between a king and a tyrant and to determine the obligations that citizens may have to the latter. His answer was that no one can appoint himself king or emperor; authority is conferred by those who are to be governed. If the sovereign breaks the implicit contract by which he was appointed by destroying what he was meant to manage, then the people are freed from their duty to obey. A tyrant can and should be removed from office.

Manegold's theory was flexible enough to avoid being stamped heretical. An implicit contract between a king and the people does not necessarily contradict the divine origin of the monarchy. On the other hand, divine authority is notably absent from the contract discussion; the church's blessing is not needed for the contract to be legitimate. When the philosophical legacy of the Greeks, via the Arabs, spread in medieval Europe, the possibility (or risk, depending on your perspective) arose that civil society could formulate laws and morals on secular grounds. Marsilius of Padua expressed this idea in *Defensor pacis* (*The Defender of Peace*), published in 1324. Marsilius argued that the power of the church has to be limited, using his non-religious interpretation of the Greek tradition as the basis of his argument. Reason and faith must be kept separate, and a life lived in accordance with a pre-Christian morality built on common sense must be sufficient for salvation. The clergy's task was reduced to teaching and offering general moral guidance. Divine power does not legitimize secular power; it stands in conflict with it, and the secular must be prioritized so it can fulfil its most important function: keeping society from falling apart.

Marsilius was way ahead of his time. Most medieval thinkers expressed themselves more carefully. Following the political infighting in the church during the 1300s, interesting contributions nevertheless did begin to surface within the Catholic camp. Nicholas of Cusa made an important contribution with *De concordantia catholica* (*The Catholic Concordance*), which was presented at the Council of Basel in the early 1430s.

What makes Nicholas's text interesting is how he handles the problem of authority in the discussion of how a consensus can be achieved in the church. His message is that consent is the foundation for all government:

> Therefore since all men are free by nature, every government that restrains its subjects from evils and uses the fear of punishment to orient their freedom toward the good, whether it consists of written laws or of a living law in the person of the prince, is constituted only by the agreement and consent of the subjects. For if by nature men are equally powerful and equally free, then the true and well-ordered authority of one who is a fellow and equal in power can only be established by the choice and consent of others, just as laws are established by consent.

## Modern Theories

When Renaissance philosophers set out to establish a new moral and political system following the medieval Scholastics, the Hellenistic tradition became their natural starting point, both in its constructive—natural justice and the social contract—and critical elements. Only one principle survived the critical review: the right to self-preservation. This idea can be found in Montaigne's essays and later in Justus Lipsius. People will seek to defend themselves, life and limb, and in doing so they are within their rights. The last important contribution before Hobbes came from Hugo Grotius, whose *De jure belli ac pacis* (*On the Law of War and Peace*) was published in 1625. Grotius's main interest was the relationship between nations, rather than between individuals, but the structure is the same and the discussion similar. He contributed to the secularization of natural law by linking it back to the Stoics and Carneades. His response to Carneades was that the common ground for all legal systems should be human nature, and that an important part of this is the yearning for a peaceful and orderly society. So, the solution to the problem does not have anything to do with Christian teachings. Grotius was even bold enough to suggest that natural law was robust enough to remain intact even if (hypothetically) there was no god. The content of natural law cannot be influenced, either, just as mathematical truths cannot be challenged.

So Thomas Hobbes was following a well-trodden path when he wrote *Leviathan*. In *De cive*, his previous book, published in 1642, he made the arrogant—and incorrect—claim that he was the founding father of political philosophy. Neither the question he asked nor the answer he offered was entirely new. But the way he asked the question and the clarity of his answer were so radical that even contemporary conservative readers who liked his conclusions were taken aback. They sensed—and rightly—that his intellectual tools could be used for other purposes and threatened to unleash uncontrollable forces. Robert Filmer, a royalist and later a target for John

Locke's criticisms, said this about *Leviathan*: "It may seem strange I should praise his building, and yet mislike his foundation; but so it is."

When it was published in 1651 in a Europe rent by religious and political conflicts, *Leviathan* established modern contract theory. Two things are important to underscore in this context. First, Hobbes's name is usually linked with authoritarian or totalitarian regimes that control not only internal and external conflicts, but also their citizens' ideas and opinions. But every contract has players, and if one player breaks the terms of the agreement, the other player is free to tear it up. Hobbes is crystal-clear on this point:

> The obligation of subjects to the sovereign is understood to last as long, and no longer, than the power lasteth by which he is able to protect them. For the right men have by nature to protect themselves, when none else can protect them, can by no covenant be relinquished. The sovereignty is the soul of the Commonwealth; which, once departed from the body, the members do no more receive their motion from it. The end of obedience is protection; which, wheresoever a man seeth it, either in his own or in another's sword, nature applieth his obedience to it, and his endeavour to maintain it. And though sovereignty, in the intention of them that make it, be immortal; yet is it in its

> own nature, not only subject to violent death
> by foreign war, but also through the ignorance
> and passions of men it hath in it, from the very
> institution, many seeds of a natural mortality,
> by intestine discord.

Simply put, Hobbes says that when the sovereign is no longer capable of upholding his part of the contract, the subjects are no longer obligated to obey, and only subjects have a say in this matter.

Also crucial is Hobbes's emphasis on people's fundamental equality. He developed the same idea we encountered in an earlier quotation from Nicholas of Cusa:

> NATURE hath made men so equal in the fac-
> ulties of body and mind as that, though there
> be found one man sometimes manifestly stron-
> ger in body or of quicker mind than another,
> yet when all is reckoned together the difference
> between man and man is not so considerable as
> that one man can thereupon claim to himself
> any benefit to which another may not pretend
> as well as he. For as to the strength of body, the
> weakest has strength enough to kill the stron-
> gest, either by secret machination or by confed-
> eracy with others that are in the same danger
> with himself.
> And as to the faculties of the mind, [. . .] I

find yet a greater equality amongst men than
that of strength.

Statements like this will hardly win you any supporters among
those who believe themselves to be the designated leaders of
society, not today and certainly not in the 1600s.

## The Liberal Response

Hobbes has been the subject of violent criticism. David Hume,
who wrote *The History of England* a century after *Leviathan*,
said:

> In our time, he is much neglected. [...] Hobbes'
> politics are fitted only to promote tyranny, and
> his ethics to encourage licentiousness. Though
> an enemy to religion, he partakes nothing of
> the spirit of scepticism, but is as positive and
> dogmatical as if human reason, and his reason
> in particular, could attain a thorough convic-
> tion in these subjects.

What came to be more important than such denunciations
was the philosophical response Hobbes's work provoked, and
which eventually grew into the liberal tradition, from John
Locke via Lord Shaftesbury, Francis Hutcheson, and David
Hume, culminating in Adam Smith and John Stuart Mill.

John Locke's philosophical work revolves around two questions: "What is knowable?" and "How should we act?" In fact, the two questions are linked, because most of all he was interested in what influences our actions. His answer has deep roots in Christianity, a religion he believed to be true, and you would expect him to lose some of his appeal among modern nonbelievers. In the second of his *Two Treatises on Government*, he even suggests that people are the property of the divine sovereign:

> . . . for men being all the workmanship of one omnipotent and infinitely wise Maker; all the servants of one sovereign Master, sent into the world by His order and about His business; they are His property, whose workmanship they are made to last during His, not one another's pleasure.

In spite of this genuinely religious framework, Locke's position as a significant thinker is widely upheld. The treatises, which constitute his most important work, are written as a direct attack on Robert Filmer, and a considerable part of Locke's argument is leveled at the absolute monarchy. The main focus of the attack is on Filmer's attempt to show that it is through divine decree that some people are put in a position to rule over others, and a great part of *The First Treatise* is taken up with showing that this kind of authority cannot be conferred by the Bible. He discusses the separation of powers, but the three pillars of power that he names are legislature, executive, and federative, of which the latter has a mainly outward-facing role in relations with other societies. The executive power is subordinate to the legislative, so in that way he is describing a form of parliamentarianism, but he does not fully develop a theory on the separation of powers, as Montesquieu would do decades later.

Even though Locke was writing in the contract tradition, he avoided the word *contract*. He preferred terms like *compact* and *trust*. The compact is the foundation of society and as such defines the relationship between the individuals who constitute it. On the other hand, a trust is not mutual; the people do not have any obligations toward the government, and a ruler's actions must always keep the citizens' best interests in mind.

His doctrine on property was more original than his critique of absolute monarchy, and it is what has secured his place in the liberal tradition. The central excerpts from *The Second Treatise* are as follows:

> Though the Earth, and all inferior Creatures, be common to all Men, yet every Man has a *Property* in his own *Person*: this no Body has any Right to but himself. The *Labour* of his Body, and the *Work* of his Hands, we may say, are properly his. Whatsoever then he removes out of the State that Nature hath provided, and left it in, he hath mixed his *Labour* with,

and joined to it something that is his own, and thereby makes it his Property. It being by him removed from the common state Nature hath placed it in, it hath by this *Labour* something annexed to it, that excludes the common right of other Men [. . .]

For 'tis *Labour* indeed that *puts the difference of value* on every thing [. . .]

The nature [of property] is, that *without a Man's own consent* it *cannot be taken from him.*

It is hardly surprising that an argument like this spoke to the aspirational bourgeoisie, who were embroiled in conflict with the landowners of the old regime, and would much later speak to the political center and right, which were eager to limit the reach of government. This doctrine might seem to conflict with the earlier idea that the Almighty Creator is the owner of all things, but for Locke, work was the way out of the state of natural equality. In a less-abstract social context, the problem remains of sharing the surplus of what has been produced through labor that involves the effort of many individuals—a problem that present-day liberals also have had to contend with.

In *The Second Treatise*, the tension between the basic freedom that is bestowed through divine grace and the limitations of freedom that might arise as a result of unequal property distribution can already be sensed. Locke opens the back door for subordination and subjection in the following passage:

> A *State* also of *Equality*, wherein all the Power and Jurisdiction is reciprocal, no one having more than another; there being nothing more evident, than that Creatures of the same species and rank promiscuously born to all the same advantages of Nature, and the use of the same faculties, should also be equal one amongst another without Subordination or Subjection, unless the Lord and Master of them all, should by any manifest Declaration of his Will set one above another, and confer on him by an evident and clear appointment an undoubted Right to Dominion and Sovereignty.

The sentence's subordinate clause comes dangerously close to the Filmerian doctrine that Locke set out to refute.

## Rousseau's Social Contract

Jean-Jacques Rousseau analyzed the social contract on two occasions: in *A Discourse Upon the Origin and the Foundation of the Inequality Among Mankind* (1755) and in *The Social Contract* (1762). The first work is primarily historical and recounts Rousseau's version of humankind's journey from its natural state to life as part of a society. In contrast to Hobbes, he deemed that life in its natural state had been pleasant and the transition into society had meant a gradual decline in quality of life. Two crucial steps in this development came with the division of labor and private ownership. The opening lines in part two of the discourse are either famous or infamous, depending on the reader's leaning:

> The first man who having enclosed a piece of land thought of saying "This is mine" and found people simple enough to believe him was the true founder of civil society. How many crimes, wars, murders, how much misery and horror the human race would have been spared if someone had pulled up the stakes and filled in the ditch and cried out to his fellow men: "Beware of this impostor: you are lost if you forget that the fruits of the earth belong to everyone and that the earth itself belongs to no one."

This passage directly contrasts Locke's idea about property. A lesser known fact is that while Rousseau was working on the above text, he was also writing an article entitled "Discourse on Political Economy" for Diderot's *Encyclopédie*, in which some of his statements could have been taken directly from Locke:

> It is certain that the right of property is the most sacred of all citizens' rights, and in some respects more important than freedom itself [. . .]

> Here we must remember that the foundation of the social pact is property, and that its first condition is that everyone should be guaranteed the peaceful enjoyment of what he owns.

These extracts are practically schizophrenic in their contradiction, and it is difficult to tell what Rousseau actually thought about ownership. The basic idea was that the social contract that provided the foundation for existent societies was false and had been forced on naive subjects by cunning rulers. In *The Social Contract*, he developed an authentic social contract that he felt was necessary for humankind to be free. Most of the book discusses constitutional democracy—government and administration, legislature, community, elections, and other building blocks. He discusses how a centralized power can be limited and notes that the best form of government varies depending on the country in question. He also discusses simple versus qualified majority rule and argues that the more important the decision, the larger the majority should be required.

The part of the doctrine that discusses the *general will* provoked the most discussion. In modern usage the term that best corresponds to it is *general interest*—an interest based on the citizens' interests, but that no one citizen feels strongly enough about to defend when thinking and acting in isolation. According to Rousseau, the problem lies in determining the general interest for any given decision-making situation. The general will cannot go wrong, but people can. He seems to have favored majority rule as the solution to the problem: ". . . the counting of votes yields a declaration of the general will." But what if no option gets a majority vote? This could occur as soon as there are more than two choices even if a simple majority is all that is required, or if there are two options and a qualified majority is needed. It is possible to get a bit further with modern voting theory, but the doctrine of general will remains a problematic segment of Rousseau's thinking.

## The Individual and the Collective

Anyone reflecting on political philosophy's fundamental problems must acknowledge the potentially destructive effect of individual impulses, passions, and self-interest. If free rein is given to such forces, life becomes intolerable for everyone around, so in some way these impulses must be contained. Saint Augustine, who defined the Catholic Church's position for some time, believed that strict inner moral control supported by external repression was the only solution. Calvin was a later representative of the same position. Conversely, Aristotle stated in classical times that as social animals (*politikon zoon*) humans are impelled to show consideration for their fellows; self-control is inherent to the human constitution. Education is the key; he who knows right acts right.

In more recent times, other alternatives have been proposed. The general consensus was that self-control would develop in one way or another, independent of external pressure or innate tendencies. It is simply assumed that controlling one's self is in the individual's interest. Early exponents can be found among the Stoics, who noted that even those who only aim to increase their wealth and power should heed social norms if they wish to succeed. Even Machiavelli, who did not ascribe any significant innate moral inhibitions to his subjects of study, claimed that keeping the good of the state as well as long-term consequences in mind forced people to control their impulses somewhat.

It was also thought that impulses and interests pull in opposite directions and neutralize each other somehow. This analogy taken from mechanics was popular with some Enlightenment philosophers such as Claude Adrien Helvétius and Baron d'Holbach, but it never spread very far.

The third alternative, which would eventually become the most important, was the idea that rules preventing society from falling apart will be developed automatically by mechanisms that are inaccessible to those involved. This is what Robert Merton once called *the theory of unanticipated consequences of purposive social action*. Representatives of the tradition include Charles-Louis de Secondat Montesquieu, Bernard Mandeville, Giambattista Vico, Adam Smith and in the twentieth century Karl Popper, Donald Campbell, and Friedrich von Hayek, among others. Within that group, the critique against Hobbes and other contract theorists is built not only on the assumption that repression is unnecessary and on knowledge-related arguments. One tries in vain to shape a society because the complex corrective mechanisms that maintain the social equilibrium cannot be understood either by those who are affected by them or by outside observers. Somewhat contradictorily, a number of proponents of these ideas have spent their fair share of time and energy trying to explain these very mechanisms.

Those who support the skeptical critics of the contract tradition often illustrate their reasoning using the market as an example. In this particular case, there are conclusions drawn from economic-welfare theory that support this argument, but the necessary assumptions are restrictive to the point of negation. The market is considered perfect, consumers are fully informed and have an unlimited capacity to process information, manufacturing and consumption have no environmental impact, and so on. Theorists like von Hayek and Milton Friedman have used examples like these to paint a general picture of harmony between individual and collective interests. There are many examples that reveal the flaws of this reasoning. Criminal behavior, environmental destruction, and segregation are all phenomena that can spontaneously arise from the drive to maximize personal welfare. By citing only positive examples, the rationality of spontaneous social development is exaggerated, a development that is further not always so spontaneous considering that individuals and powerful groups can influence the direction it takes.

What this doctrine conveys, at least in its pared-down and

popularized form, is that self-interest is a sufficient guiding principle in society. This is the answer to the Hobbesian provocation that uncontrolled self-interest, in the best case, leads to an infertile stasis, or at worst, to civil war. Both Hobbes and his critics were liberals in the sense that to them the individual was an obvious starting point for questions of morality and politics. Their assumptions about what drives people's actions were not radically different, so to find the answer to the question of why they arrived at different conclusions, we must look elsewhere.

## Modern Analytical Versions

In December 1954, Richard Braithwaite delivered his inaugural lecture in moral philosophy at Cambridge: *The Theory of Games as a Tool for the Moral Philosopher.* It marked the start of a fruitful collaboration between philosophers and mathematicians. He showed that a number of typical problems of choice that had preoccupied moral philosophers could be mapped onto simple games that had been analyzed in game theory, which at this point was still in its early phases.

The development of game theory during the second half of the twentieth century led to renewed interest in formalized versions of philosophical dilemmas. For contract theory, two situations were of particular interest. The first concerns signing the social contract. If it is assumed that a number of people acting in their own self-interest are discussing entering into a social contract, who is to say that they are interested in signing one at all? In a way, the question relates to the biological discussion about the origin of social behavior among animals. In the 1980s, Robert Axelrod popularized this approach to such an extent that for many, signing a social contract began to seem superfluous. Now, the conditions of cooperative solutions are not as good as Axelrod suggested, primarily because he only focused on interactions between two players, and the majority of social interactions that people participate in take place in larger groups—often much larger. The results of games with only two players cannot be generalized.

The other branch, which gained momentum in the 1970s, is about the type of social contract that does get signed, if it is assumed that there is actually an interest in doing so. John Rawls proposed a new variation of contract theory in his book *A Theory of Justice*, which provoked a response from Robert Nozick, *Anarchy, State, and Utopia*, also using contract theory's terminology. Rawls thought that the individuals who analyze different forms of the contract in the imaginary contract situation would act with caution and choose a version of the contract that gives the best possible outcome for those who have it worst in this future society. Nozick responded by questioning the very design of Rawls's contract. Rawls's theory builds on an assessment of the social outcomes on the basis of certain norms. Theories built on what Nozick calls "historical principles" focus on what has led to the social condition at a given point in time. Within this category, one can then differentiate between those that are built on a certain theory of distribution—for instance, "to each according to their need"—and those that do not. Nozick's own alternative belongs to the second group. His theory is entirely procedural in that conditions that are the result of legitimate processes are considered legitimate.

At a certain remove from the controversy, the economist John Harsanyi presented a modernized utilitarian version of contract theory. Harsanyi's analysis yields a less equal solution, falling somewhere between Rawls and Nozick. Later, Ken Binmore, another economist, tried to bring order to the discussion in a series of books. Binmore's work is without a doubt one of the most ambitious attempts to establish a solid foundation for contract theory using rational-actor models. Binmore concludes that the players involved in the contract would come to an egalitarian solution, but for reasons other than the ones Rawls's proposed. We will come back to this in the next chapter.

## The Social Contract—and Then What?

It is no coincidence that the idea of the social contract has had such appeal over the centuries. Those who do not accept a moral or political system based on religion, myth, or the status quo really do not have any choice but to take a rational approach—which society would we choose if we could liberate ourselves from the one we have today? Critics of the contract—Hume, von Hayek, and others—usually acknowledge the need for a constitution, and a constitution is essentially a type of social contract. It is another matter that most constitutions historically have come into existence under completely different circumstances than the ideal contract situation that philosophers have been using as a model.

What is striking about the many contributions to political philosophy is their similarity in reasoning, right across ideological lines. Even if one accepts Nozick's categorization in end-result and historical theories, it can be said that they all are more or less built on an implicit contract theory: the author presents theories that are recommended starting points for society-building and that are expected to last for eternity.

Among the many commonalities of the various political philosophers' hypotheses, they all share the same obvious blind spot. Like the tale in Sigfrid Lindström's poem, their story ends where the real story begins. What happens when the contract is signed and everyday life begins, filled with human shortcomings, war, and natural disasters? Only then are fundamental principles put to their test. For the purposes of this discussion—that of inequality—the ultimate test of a theory's durability is how it weathers the inherent instability described in previous chapters. If the egalitarian starting point assumed by the signatories at the time of signing the contract will not survive for very long, then how these ideologies propose to manage this instability should be the test of their intellectual rigor. This is the topic of the following three chapters.

# 7

## LIBERALISM AND INEQUALITY

*The common task liberal thinkers have set themselves is the shaping of a good constitution that will regulate the relationship between individuals—and between individuals and the state.*

Liberalism, conservatism, and socialism, the three major Western ideological currents, of course represent completely different attitudes to the question of inequality. Certain thinkers, particularly those on the right, have tried to strike equality from the political agenda, but most have taken it seriously. In this and the following chapters, we will take a closer look at how the classical ideologies have related to inequality as a problem. Before we continue, let us summarize the main points of our analyses of the origin of inequality so far:

+ The fundamental symmetrical equilibrium in the elementary bargaining game is unstable. In other words, even if we begin with an equal starting point, there will be small disruptions in this balance that will intensify and soon lead to unequal distribution. There is no other equilibrium. Inequality is only limited by the external restrictions of the game—either the stronger player wants to keep the weaker alive and reasonably productive, or the weaker player can leave the game or find other options.

+ Chance determines who, in practice, gets the upper hand in a situation where effort and talent are identical.

+ Traditions and inheritance laws reinforce inequality, but they do not for that reason legitimate it.

+ Feedback from actual social and economic outcomes makes it possible to stabilize a society at a reasonable level of equality. Feedback is crucial in addressing the inherent instability of the bargaining dynamic. Even with feedback, inequality cannot be eliminated completely.

A number of test cases can be used when investigating to what extent various ideologies are prepared to accept the status quo as the norm. For instance, one can look at the position of women in society and how the oppression of the female half of the population has been accepted or even condoned by ideological and religious systems. But here we will use slavery, an institution that infringes on the most fundamental conditions of equality, if we imagine that we are starting from a relatively equal place of origin, whether it is shrouded in religious mythology or is built on the idea of a social contract.

## The Contours of Liberalism

Like other broad ideological terms, *liberalism* is hard to define. The term itself is relatively new—it started to be used in early nineteenth-century Spain—but the concept is, of course, much older. Writers as disparate as Locke, Smith, Mill, Keynes and von Hayek fall under the rubric of liberalism. The latter, whom many would consider a conservative, was so intent on being identified as a liberal that he appended to his book *The Constitution of Liberty* an essay titled "Why I Am Not a Conservative." Two of the main opponents in the political-philosophical debate in the 1970s, John Rawls and Robert Nozick, maintained that they were liberals, too.

Liberalism tends to be defined in opposition to the values and terms of the old regime. Liberals believe that reason, not tradition, should be the basis for all social institutions, and that any institutions and customs that do not pass the test of reason should be dismantled. Relationships between individuals in a society should be based on rationally grounded contracts rather than on status, if status is not based on objective merits. Liberalism turns its gaze to the present and the future, while the ideology of the old regime looks to the past.

As Anthony Arblaster states in his analysis of the liberal

tradition, liberalism is more than a set of values. Liberalism strives for a scientific worldview. A key starting point is individualism, which takes various forms. The first is *ontological* individualism, the idea that people *are* essentially alone. Then there is *political* individualism, which appeared as early as the seventeenth century among thinkers such as Hobbes and Spinoza, and which posits the individual—not the family, society, or any other superindividual entity—as the basic unit of political theory. These types of individualism were complemented in the twentieth century by the *methodological* individualism of Popper and other thinkers, which, in short, means that within the social sciences the individual is taken as the starting point for the analysis of social processes.

Of course, individualism was not born in the 1600s. Medieval historians like Alan Macfarlane and Emmanuel Le Roy Ladurie have reported fully developed individualistic ways of thinking and behavioral patterns much earlier, and the same is found in classical Greek dramas, even if one must be careful when interpreting documents from another time. But it would be correct to say that with the dawn of the new age individualism grew both ideologically and philosophically.

The individualist perspective and emphasis on formal relationships make liberalism compatible with the social contract as a model in political theory. As stated, basing a political philosophy on a hypothetical social contract is nothing new, but it is no coincidence that this school of thought was enriched with some of its most significant contributions during the epoch of classical liberalism. Liberal thinkers have set themselves the task of shaping a good constitution that will regulate the relationship between individuals and also between individuals and the state. Key building blocks include a number of rights, such as equality in the eyes of the law, freedom of expression, freedom to assemble, and property rights.

What differentiates liberals are the alternatives that they imagine there are to ordered life in civil society. If, like Hobbes, one believes that the alternative is constant conflict and general insecurity—metaphorically summarized as a state of war "where every man is enemy to every man"—it is easy to accept a far-reaching justification for state intervention in the lives of its citizens. On the other hand, if you believe in self-organizing processes in society, it follows on that you would want to limit the state's ability to intervene. This is the critical point at which various currents within liberalism part ways.

## The Absence of a Stable Equilibrium

Liberalism's goal of drafting the ideal constitution is underpinned by the optimistic assumption that a project like this can actually be realized. In a key passage in *Anarchy, State, and Utopia*, Nozick makes the previously mentioned distinction between historical principles of justice and those that are based on actual end-results. Historical principles are based on the idea that "past circumstances or actions of people can create differential entitlement or differential deserts to things." The other type of principle refers to the actual state of society and evaluates it in relation to a theory of justice. Nozick also calls the second kind *patterned principles*, because they build on a natural dimension or combination of dimensions—merit, need, marginal productivity, etc.

Few liberals have suggested that any of these principles alone constitutes a complete solution to the distribution problem. Nozick is an exception, suggesting that historical principles are the only just basis for distribution. An owner has the right to keep whatever she has obtained in accordance to the basic rules and regulations, on the condition that the constitution has been arrived at fairly. Taxation, according to Nozick, is on a par with forced labor.

Nozick's argument for historical principles can be evaluated using the conclusions from the previous chapters. There are two problems: the formulation of constitutional rules that are meant to provide a foundation for rights, and the absence of feedback from society. The first problem is comparable with drafting a moral theory or code of conduct; the goal is to describe rules applicable to any given scenario that could lead to good or at the very least adequate outcomes. Referring to some authoritative text of religious or quasi-religious origin is unacceptable in a modern liberal context. As such, the only option is to evaluate proposed rules according to the impact they have in a social context. But a trial period is finite by definition, which means that there is always an element of uncertainty when making rules. As in the examples of the Catholic Church and the nobility in Chapter 5, there is a good chance that mistakes be made when the rules are drafted, and so if citizens have on principle abdicated the right to change the constitution, there is no way to correct these mistakes.

Even more problematic when shaping the ideal constitution is the unstable outcome discussed in previous chapters. To use the language of control systems engineering, the search for the perfect constitution is equivalent to trying to control a process without having information about its actual performance; that is, based only on feedforward. Even in a stable system this is bound to fail; the system will keep working unchecked and end up far from a desirable—or even acceptable—outcome in the long run. When the experiment is conducted in an unstable system like the elementary bargaining game we know from previous chapters, the result can be disastrous if judged by current moral or political norms. Again, Nozick takes an extreme position by not excluding slavery, which is one possible outcome if the mechanisms that the constitution is built on are allowed to run unchecked:

> The comparable question about an individual
> is whether a free system will allow him to sell
> himself into slavery. I believe that it would.

Nozick hastens to add that a free system would also allow him to commit to never entering into such a transaction. However, this is an empty restriction because every self-imposed commitment can be rescinded and undoubtedly would be by individuals in dire enough straits, as history has shown on numerous occasions.

In summary, one must either relinquish the idea of a perfect constitution and allow for feedback from society or refrain from putting any restrictions on the conditions deemed acceptable, for example prohibiting slavery. Few would follow in Nozick's footsteps and choose the latter option. Among liberal thinkers who are still trying to draft the perfect constitution, the normal assumption should be that other civilized social equilibria can be found between the original egalitarian equilibrium and the unfettered exploitation of our fellow human beings. As has been shown, the basic bargaining game does not have such an equilibrium.

There is in fact strong tension between liberals like Nozick, who try to draft the perfect constitution based on rights, and other liberals like von Hayek and Popper, who emphasize the need for continual adaptions and adjustments in the rules that help guide a society—*piecemeal social engineering*, in Popper's words. The first group tends to think in the tradition of the social contract, while the other avoids or abhors it. The practical political conclusions will not necessarily be very different, but as far as intellectual foundations go, you cannot have it both ways; you have to choose. Most liberals would probably choose the second, pragmatic alternative and open the door for continual social feedback on the framework that will be used in governing society. The discussion, then, is no longer about whether or not feedback like this is appropriate or necessary, but what the feedback mechanism itself should look like.

# Questions of Legitimacy

The liberal doctrine of legitimacy bears the stamp of John Locke. Property, liberty, and security for life and limb are the chief values that should be protected by the state. Property is earned; the right to property is conveyed through various types of effort. The modern liberal thinker Wojciech Sadurski offers a morally tinged definition of what "earned" means, and so deviates from Nozick's theory about rights. Sadurski suggests that gains must be connected to responsibility; a person can gain property only through actions for which he can also be held responsible. This implies a significant refinement of the demands of legitimacy. The economist Frank Knight once noted: "The ownership of personal or material productive capacity is based upon a complex mixture of inheritance, luck, and effort, probably in that order of relative importance." Property acquired through inheritance or by chance is not legitimate in Sadurski's definition.

One conclusion of the analysis in previous chapters is that chance and history are two main factors behind the distribution of wealth in the bargaining game. Historical legacy is not a basis for legitimacy in mainstream liberal thought; liberalism arose in part in opposition to inherited rights and privileges. The fact that the portion that goes to one player in a negotiation at a certain time tends to increase over time only because it was larger at some point in the past is, therefore, a serious threat to the legitimacy of distribution.

That is not to say that effort does not matter; the relative importance of chance, inheritance, effort, and other factors is an issue that warrants its own investigation. On a global level, the economist Branko Milanović has calculated the relative importance of a person's general background and family along with individual factors (chance and effort) to their earnings. His conclusion is clear: more than 80 percent of a person's real income will depend on circumstances beyond her control: country of birth and family background. One objection to this idea is that family influence can, to an extent, be passed on through behavioral patterns that are in some way connected to effort, but whatever the effect, it is small. Additionally, the element of chance contributes to the remaining 20 percent, which by definition is beyond an individual's control. Milanović's analysis confirms Knight's guess.

Simple thought experiments help cast doubt on the reigning distribution of wealth. For example, relocate an average CEO from a European or American company to an average developing nation in Central Africa. What would happen to his (it is most often a man) productivity? The answer is that it would be drastically reduced because the result of his efforts is decided to a large extent by social factors—the employees' level of education, their engagement in their work, the quality of the infrastructure, and so on. The results of a CEO's efforts are, as with all others who are working in an integrated economy built on a division of labor, socially determined.

The same kind of comparisons can be made over time. In 1965, the average American CEO in a larger company earned 24 times as much as the average worker. In 2005, this number had risen to 262. In Sweden, this quotient has been measured since 1950, when it was 26. In 1980, it was at its lowest (9), only to rise to 46 in 2011. A CEO's productivity is hard to compare to a worker's, but no one can seriously claim that this number, relatively speaking, could have grown more than tenfold in forty years, as is the case in the United States. The fluctuations in Sweden are a strong indication that salaries and productivity are only weakly correlated; salaries are socially determined. The conclusion is the same: prevailing patterns of distribution constitute a serious threat to legitimacy, per the liberal definition.

## Liberalism and the Politics of Redistribution

Among conscientious English liberals, there is a "tendency toward equality," as Anthony Trollope once noted. This tendency is built into liberalism to an extent, because contract theory is anonymous and neutral between individuals. Reactions have varied when the ideology has had to address actual inequalities resulting from liberalism in practice. Left liberals, or "social liberals," as they often call themselves, are prepared to use the state's tools of power to correct breaches of reasonable norms of justice. Others have been wary or openly hostile to the idea of using public power for these purposes.

Differences between individuals are often divided into three categories: those that depend on innate traits, on differences in background, and on outcomes. It is often thought that the first category is difficult to influence. A measure of caution must be observed when calling a trait "genetically determined." The expression of genes can be influenced by environmental factors before birth, which could very well be influenced by political intervention. In his doctoral thesis, for instance, Peter Nilsson, a researcher at Uppsala University, showed that people who were exposed to alcohol before birth performed worse in school, earned less, and were more dependent on welfare at the age of thirty than those who were not exposed to alcohol. In their controversial book *The Bell Curve: Intelligence and Class Structure in American Life*, Richard Herrnstein and Charles Murray argue that an individual's talents are largely set at birth and that this talent can be measured with an IQ test. With this we see that even successful, high-level academics have a hard time differentiating between genetically determined differences and those due to schooling and the social milieu.

As far as the other types of difference go, most liberal writers agree that individuals should be given fairly equal opportunities in life—it's talent and effort that should be rewarded—but opinions are divided on how active the state should be in compensating for differences rooted in social background. Among liberals there is a greater consensus that differences in the third category (outcome) should not be offset.

Among modern liberal thinkers, John Rawls is one of the most outspoken proponents of an active distribution policy. His second principle of justice states: "Social and economic inequalities are to be arranged so that they are both (a) to the greatest expected benefit of the least advantaged and (b) attached to offices and positions open to all under conditions of fair equality of opportunity." This statement has been hailed as a basis for liberal equalization policies, but exactly how active the state's role should be within the framework of such a program is open to discussion. The answer is highly dependent on the time frame. For the short-sighted viewer, principle (a) is essentially an argument for complete eradication of difference. A transfer that elevates the people with the worst lot to the same level as those who are just above them leads to an outcome that is better for those who are worst off, and it should be implemented. Using the same argument, the two who are now in the lowest positions will move to the next-highest level. Repeated use of the same argument leads to the conclusion that equalization is the only acceptable arrangement.

The long-term situation is different; taxes put toward aiding redistribution can have an effect on the labor supply, savings, and other important variables, so a policy that is also the best for those who are worst off can presuppose differences in income and assets. On the other hand, the adequacy of a given time frame depends on people's ability to sustain themselves—those who are worse off usually have a shorter time horizon—and so here we face a genuine political problem.

Rawls's theory of justice has given rise to a number of predictable responses from various camps—communitarians critical of his unwavering individualistic perspective, critiques of not respecting property rights from conservative liberals and conservatives, among others—which are of limited relevance to this discussion. But a more technical criticism is leveled by researchers such as John Harsanyi and Ken Binmore. Rawls's theory is grounded in rationality. The bridge principle (see the end of Chapter 4) that he uses to move from facts to recommendations is rationality. He suggests that the path he recommends is what rational individuals in a contract situation would choose. More precisely, he uses the so-called *maximin criterion*, a decision criterion that means that the people designing a contract would choose a solution that gives the best possible worst-case scenario. This is connected to principle (a) above, which states that society should be ordered so that those who are worst off can have as the best possible outcome. Rawls's argument is that the individuals who consider signing the social contract would choose that principle to be sure that they would not have to face truly regrettable future outcomes.

Rawls's argument represents a form of insurance thinking. When we are to choose between different options and cannot with any certainty predict what the various alternatives will lead to, we must imagine ourselves in various situations. Perhaps this would resemble the table below, where the numbers show the value of the various outcomes.

|          | Scenario 1 | Scenario 2 |
|----------|------------|------------|
| Option A | 5          | 1          |
| Option B | 7          | −1         |

If Scenario 1 occurs, Option B is preferable. But if it's Scenario 2, then Option A is better. If you want to be certain that you're avoiding the worst option, you should choose Option A. If you could determine the likelihood of the two scenarios, then the analysis can go a bit deeper. The more likely Scenario 1 is, the better a choice Option B is. If a calculation shows that the likelihood of Scenario 1 is greater than 50 percent, then Option B is preferable. According to the expected utility hypothesis, Option B should be chosen as soon as you think you know the likelihood is greater than 50 percent. But if $-1$ seems like an unacceptable outcome, you should still choose Option A.

Harsanyi calls Rawls's insurance thinking "highly irrational" and believes that it leads to "absurd practical implications." For Harsanyi, expected utility is the only acceptable criterion. What he and those who are like-minded mean is that there is no human progress without risk. But he is wrong in claiming that this is irrational. If the negative outcome in the table above is considered unacceptable, it is necessary to choose Option A. A homeowner buying home insurance already knows that the cost of the premium exceeds the expected payout; otherwise, the insurance company could not exist. And yet, home insurance policies are sold for the simple reason that no one wants to experience the worst-case scenario—being left with nothing.

In his own analysis, Harsanyi bans what he calls "antisocial preferences," including envy, and ascribes the freedom to choose an unknown (but apparently high) value. The solution that he eventually arrives at is a slightly modernized version of classical utilitarianism in moral theory. Harsanyi's cherry-picking among human weaknesses—greediness is acceptable and even commendable, while envy is reprehensible—undermines both his own and his subject's academic credibility.

Binmore agrees with Harsanyi about the idea that rational decision-makers should base their choices on expected utility. He claims that the maximin principle cannot be reconciled with rationality, but his reasoning differs from Harsanyi's. Binmore rejects every form of external coercion, whether or not it concerns guiding moral principles like natural law, Kant's categorical imperative, or a government of Hobbes's design. By doing this he eliminates every option but equality; it is the only one that all people would accept in advance, on the condition that coercion is not allowed. According to Binmore, Rawls came to the right conclusion on the wrong grounds. But Binmore's own requirement that there be a total lack of coercion is far too strict to be generally applicable.

Both Harsanyi and Binmore are rather too quick to reject the maximin principle as a guide when making complex decisions. It may be true that expected utility can work well when making everyday decisions that will only marginally impact individual welfare, but it does not necessarily apply to the big decisions that can impact a person's entire future. For the theory of expected utility to exist, certain general conditions have to be met, such as being able to objectively determine the likelihood of various outcomes. This doesn't apply to the contract situation, and so economic utility theory cannot be applied. When making a choice like that, a more cautious decision-making strategy like the maximin principle might in fact be more rational.

The problem for all participants in the discussion—Rawls, Harsanyi, Binmore, and others—is that there is no one decision rule that can be claimed to be the only rational one. Rationality is far too weak a bridge principle to be used to draw general conclusions about the content of the social contract. And so liberalism itself has no answer to the question of distribution. To the extent that distributional issues are addressed, they will have to build on an external morality.

## The Value of Variety

Although many liberal thinkers seem to have neglected problems of inequality due to oversight or perhaps to lack of interest, some have stressed the positive value of difference. Wilhelm von Humboldt is an early representative of this line of thought:

> The spirit of the Government prevails in all such institutions, and however wise and salutary such a spirit may be, it nevertheless produces uniformity and an alien mode of behavior in the nation. [. . .] The greatest gift society can bestow lies just in the very diversity arising out of such an association of several people; and this diversity is invariably forfeited in proportion to the degree of State interference.

In his classic text *Democracy in America*, Alexis de Tocqueville identifies the pros of democracy as well as its cons—

summarized in his term the *tyranny of the majority*. John Stuart Mill was influenced by de Tocqueville and moved away from direct democracy and toward representative democracy. Mill wanted to protect the individual from all forms of social pressure, whether enacted directly or by the state:

> But the strongest of all the arguments against
> the interference of the public with purely per-
> sonal conduct, is that when it does interfere,
> the odds are that it interferes wrongly, and in
> the wrong place.

Mill also made sure to advocate for the protection of the intellectual elite, who he deemed essential to good governance. He was opposed to progressive taxation, because he felt that it punished those who work harder and save more than others. A more modern and more technical version of that thought can be found with Joseph Schumpeter, who was particularly interested in the mechanisms of the capitalist system that tend to undermine its very foundation.

Even though each of these arguments contains a seed of truth, they are weak arguments against the necessity of offsetting vast differences in the distribution of welfare. It is true that certain differences in income and capital stem from differences in talent and effort, but as has been made clear, most do not. Besides, there are no guarantees that a ruling elite will use their greater-than-average influence over the management of a country in support of the public interest. For most ruling elites throughout history, whether democratically elected or not, staying in power is their primary goal, and public interest is at best been a means to this end. It is highly unlikely that the signatories of the social contract would acknowledge this to be a significant argument for inequality.

# 8

## CONSERVATISM: INEQUALITY AS A NECESSITY AND AN ASSET

*Custom is the mother of legitimacy.*

If liberalism is hard to define and summarize, the plethora of ideas that fall under the banner of conservatism are even more so. Some versions of conservatism are religious, while others are agnostic or atheist. Using a broad interpretation of the term, both old and modern theocracies rely on forms of conservatism. Early-modern conservative thinkers such as David Hume and Edmund Burke wrote within the framework of the Enlightenment, whereas early-nineteenth-century conservatives were part of the Counter-Enlightenment. Some conservatives have argued that the state should support social institutions, such as the nuclear family; others have tried to limit the state's reach using the same arguments that von Humboldt and Mill used. Both protectionists and those in favor of free trade can be found in the conservative camp. The list goes on. Nevertheless, there are recurring themes in conservative thinking that make it possible to relate conservatism to our previous conclusions.

Fundamentally, *knowledge skepticism* characterizes conservatism. This skepticism has taken various forms over the centuries, from the general skepticism cultivated by Hume via the religious or mystical institutional arguments of Burke and Joseph de Maistre to modern variations of von Hayek and Popper (though the latter would probably have defended himself against the epithet "conservative"). One unifying factor is the emphasis on human ignorance as it pertains to fundamental social processes, which is used to legitimate the status quo and to question proposed reforms. The idea that a social contract could be made by a hypothetical group of people in a pre-social stage is considered a ridiculous or simply dangerous idea. Hume was afraid that contract theories could undermine the legitimacy of existing regimes, and Burke harbored similar misgivings.

There is also skepticism about the individual as the starting point in the construction of social and political theories. These critics of individualism can also be found outside the conservative camp, among nineteenth-century French authors such as Balzac, Sainte-Beuve, and Lamartine, and also among modern communitarian thinkers. Concurrently, conservative writers often defend the individual in the political debate, preferring to reduce the political problem to a tug-of-war between the individual and the state. This leads to the misuse of the term *individual*, such as when the word is used to describe a business with economic and legal resources that are comparable to those of an average-size country. In the showdown between such legal entities and the state, the outcome is far from a given.

A third shared trait is the consensus on religion's role in creating social stability, though opinions on the truth of religion vary. Some believe religions to be true and therefore a natural (or indeed, obvious) basis for society's moral order. Others are more interested in the instrumental value of religion; their utility is more important than their degree of truthfulness. The latter argument is not usually spoken about openly, because it risks being self-defeating.

## The Absence of a Stable Equilibrium

At first, the conclusion of the analysis of the bargaining game—that there is no stable egalitarian equilibrium—might seem to confirm the conservative view that equality is impossible, what Albert Hirschman called the *futility argument*. This idea has long been central to conservative thought and is found in the work of theorists as varied as the early-twentieth-century classical Italian sociologists Gaetano Mosca and Vilfredo Pareto and present-day social scientists Kenneth Boulding and Nathan Keyfitz. Nevertheless, inequality is a question of degree, so the status quo needs further justification. On this point, conservatives diverge.

In fact, the lack of stable equilibria that fulfill reasonable moral demands in the bargaining game might be problematic for conservative thinkers. Whether it will or not be depends on which outcomes of social interaction one is prepared to accept. Generally, conservative writers have been more likely than others to accept what most would spontaneously reject on moral grounds, such as the oppression of women and slavery. They have often done this with reference to tradition, local customs, or property rights.

There is continuity in the critical (and sometimes ironic) attitude of conservatives commenting on well-meaning but (allegedly) unrealistic stances of political reformers throughout history. They emphasize the importance of institutions to personal welfare and argue that the survival of these institutions is being threatened by ignorant reformers. Today's conservatives are not likely to accept slavery as an institution, but Nozick did, and he was not alone among twentieth-century theorists.

## The Problem of Legitimacy

Conservatism inherits a large share of liberalism's legitimacy problem. Few of today's Western conservatives look exclusively to the past in order to legitimate an imbalanced distribution of society's resources; instead, they refer to present-day contributions of those with capital and high salaries. And so we are faced with the same argument that was lodged against liberalism in the previous chapter. But conservatism also has other, more regressive lines of argument. Taking a global view, it is necessary to look at conservatism in the context of the history of ideas and religion.

When chance plays as big a role in social development as has been suggested here, the defenders of the status quo face a significant legitimacy problem. If minor changes a few generations back determined who ended up with the upper hand and these differences were exacerbated as a direct result of social interaction, it is unclear what the economic elite are basing their claims on. Legitimacy has been the main conundrum for both those in power and conservative thinkers, then as now. Various solutions have been sought. If you disregard democracy as a means of achieving legitimacy, then those in power can gain legitimacy through what they *do* or what they *are*. To do something—to perform a service in exchange for taxes and subservience—is the safer option, whether it is about contact with the gods, protection from outside enemies, or upholding law and order. One attractive option is to base authority on the achievements of past generations, and to connect it with a transfer mechanism (inheritance or apostolic succession, for instance), which can ensure continuity. The farther back in time this basis can be located, the greater chance there is of allowing history to become legend or myth, beyond criticism. For Plato, the end point in this process was the noble lie—noble (*gennaios*) because it was the foundation of the social order.

Historically and globally, the most significant solution has been to use religion as support. Joseph de Maistre was uncommonly clear about his solution to the legitimacy problem when he wrote, "The more divine the basis of an institution, the more durable it is" and "If therefore you wish to *conserve* all, *consecrate* all." Throughout history, this idea has been the basis for many alliances between secular and religious leaders, where the latter were invited to share the power in exchange for legitimizing the former. This solution becomes especially stable when the reigning power structure can be traced back to old religious documents; when their origin is lost in the shadows of history, one can claim that their origin is in fact divine.

In theory, the clergy has an advantage because its power stems from the gods, but this can be different in practice. Gods rarely meddle directly in the affairs of human beings, and the monopoly on organized violence that secular rulers have gives them a strong card to play in negotiations. As history shows, the outcome is not always predictable.

The following examples taken from the great world religions will help illustrate the attempt to solve the legitimacy problem on religious grounds. There are striking similarities between the various religions both in the problems that have arisen and in the solutions that have been proposed.

## Religious Foundations: Hinduism

Early Indian history is recounted in one of two ways. In the traditional version, the Indian subcontinent was invaded from the northwest some time during the second millennium BCE, when it was populated by people who spoke Dravidian languages. The intruders introduced a strict hierarchical social order—the seeds of the caste system. Their main problem, aside from legitimacy, was the lack of women, which made it necessary to allow for women's upward social mobility. The other historical account, put forth by nationalist representatives of society's upper strata, is that the social stratification originated in a native culture that had roots in the Indus Valley civilization several thousand years before the alleged invasion.

If not for DNA profiling, this ideological battle would most likely never have been resolved. In 2001, an Indian-American research team published the results of their comparison between mitochondrial DNA and Y-chromosomes from Indians and equivalent samples from African, European, and other Asian individuals. The results were striking. The DNA from the maternal lineage is closer to Asian DNA, but similarities with European DNA increase the higher up in the castes one goes. As for the DNA from the paternal lineage, the similarity with European samples is generally greater, also here with greater similarities higher up in the caste system. This picture supports the traditional story about an invading male-dominated Indo-European people who established themselves as the leaders of society, preventing upward social mobility among men but allowing a certain degree of mobility for women. But this is new information, and its impact on the legitimacy of the Indian social structure remains to be seen. So far, the traditional legitimation stands, and it is religious in nature.

In Hinduism, the blueprint for a good society is found in *The Laws of Manu*. A rough description can be found in the classic texts *Rig Veda* and *Bhagavad Gita*, which were probably compiled between 1500 and 1000 BCE. A more conclusive form is said to have been recorded by the great Manu and forwarded by his students and followers, finally finding its definitive form during the first or second century. The work is composed of about 2,700 verses collected in twelve books, which were given the name *Manusmrti*, or *Manavadharmashastra* in Sanskrit. The word *manava* is the genitive of Manu, but it also means *human*. As such, the other form can, somewhat haughtily, be interpreted as "The Laws of Humanity."

*The Laws of Manu* is an example of a type of political philosophy that defines an ideal society down to the very last detail—what should and should not be eaten, whom to marry, crime and punishment, a woman's place in society, and so forth. Like Plato's *Republic*, with which it shares some elements, it describes an ideal state and an order of things that should prevail so that society does not slip into chaos.

The world that the text describes is deeply characterized by violence. Modern readers might be reminded of social-Darwinist texts from the late nineteenth century, and simple ones at that. There are two options: eat or be eaten. The result is a zero-sum vision of society, in which every person's gain is another's loss. In a society like that, there is hardly room for cooperation or progress.

One of the central metaphors is that society (*varna*) is a human body. The religious elite (*brahmin*) are the head, the warriors (*kshatriya*) the arms, tradespeople and craftspeople (*vaishya*) are the thighs, and finally the servants (*shudra*) are the feet. Combined with the idea that everything below the waist is impure, an immutable division of people into higher and lower positions is established—a division that cannot be changed because the human body is the way it is. Another concept, the transmigration of the soul, completes this construct. The suggestion that all people get what they deserve as a result of their actions in a previous life—an assertion that can neither be confirmed nor refuted—is a clever concept, politically speaking. A person with high standing has been rewarded for previous good deeds; an untouchable at the bottom of society has behaved badly; otherwise they would not be where they are today. It is hard to imagine a more powerful affirmation of the status quo.

There is a natural tension between the two highest castes: the priests and warriors. The religious elite have seldom contented themselves with having monopoly on contact with the spiritual realm, and has also laid claim to secular power. Some of the demands that are presented in *The Laws of Manu* are anything but ethereal:

> For when a priest is born he is born at the top of the earth, as the lord of all living beings, to guard the treasure of religion. All of this belongs to the priest, whatever there is in the universe; the priest deserves all of this because of his excellence and high birth. The priest eats only

what is his own, he wears what is his own, and he gives what is his own; other people eat through the priests' mercy.

[. . .]

And when a learned priest finds a treasure that was previously hidden, he may take it even without leaving anything, for he is the overlord of everything.

The culture that resulted from the fusion of the native population and the Indo-European invaders seems to have been established around 1000 BCE. The first sacred text, *Rig Veda*, is the ideological confirmation of this. Following a common pattern, the elite gradually lost their hold, and in the 500s Buddhism and Jainism quickly emerged as religious alternatives. They were created among the same ruling and political elite that supported the dominant belief system, which in itself is a sign of social disintegration. Another five hundred years later, the time was ripe for a Brahminic renaissance. Hinduism emerged as a renewed form of Brahminism and was codified in *The Laws of Manu*. Tax revenue that had previously gone to Buddhist monasteries was being redirected to Brahminist groups. Buddhist centers gradually lost their influence, so as Buddhism grew into a significant religious and social power in Central and East Asia, its survival was being threatened in its country of origin. Since the Brahmins gained control over the

administration of justice, using a method of local conflict resolution reminiscent of the one practiced in Muslim countries,
their position was also strengthened against the warrior caste.

In time, the various social implications of both religions
became clearer. Both Hinduism and Buddhism were originally compatible with the caste system. In Buddhism, this
was mainly achieved by shifting the focus away from this
world. Gradually, Buddhism became more egalitarian and began to stand in greater conflict with the class system. When
it seemed likely that India would gain independence during
the first half of the twentieth century, a carefully considered
strategy was needed to address the social legacy of the caste
system. Hindu traditionalists, who had the strongest foothold
in the upper castes, preached a return to pre-colonial values.
Another faction, to which Mohandas Gandhi belonged, believed the caste system to be an integral part of Indian culture,
but tried to reconcile it with an egalitarian view of humanity.
They held that caste affiliation should not constitute a legitimate basis for valuing one person more highly than another.
Gandhi planned to use the caste system's categories as instruments to increase social and economic equality in the country,
a strategy that proved to be less successful.

The third faction was staunchly against the caste system.
The most brilliant example among them was Bhimrao Ramji
Ambedkar, who was himself from an untouchable caste. He
earned his doctorate in sociology from Columbia University
in 1917 and then returned to India to take up the fight against
what he believed to be a shameful institution. In 1927, Ambed-

kar caused controversy by publicly burning a copy of *The Laws of Manu*. He officially left Hinduism in 1956 and became a Buddhist; many untouchables followed him, eliciting nervous reactions from Hindu leaders.

At the cusp of the 2000s, history repeated itself. Ambedkar's followers began to spread his appeal again and a certain response came in the form of people converting to Buddhism. As a countermeasure, Hindu leaders offered converts a higher position in the caste system if they returned to their old religion. Apparently, the sacred social order is negotiable.

## Religious Foundations: Christianity

Christianity originally cultivated a different relationship to secular power than that cultivated by Hinduism. Whereas Hinduism evolved specifically to legitimate a power structure imposed by an invading warrior caste, Christianity initially occupied a disempowered position and went on to become the dominant faith in the areas to which it spread. This success can be attributed to how the religious leaders skillfully adapted themselves to the secular powers with whom they were interacting.

The key figures in this early development, Jeshua (Jesus) and Shaul (Paul), were careful not to provoke Roman authorities. Of course, Jeshua's views are only available to us in the edited form found in the gospels, where the ethereality of his word is underscored: "My kingdom is not of this world." The message is summarized with this efficient and malleable advice: "Render unto Caesar the things that are Caesar's, and unto God the things that are God's."

The gospel of Paul is more developed on this point, possibly because it was created specifically to defuse the dangerous connection between religious devotion and Jewish nationalism. Paul's letter to the Romans established what would become a cornerstone in the despotic monarchy's argument for the divine right of kings:

> Let every soul be subject unto the higher powers. For there is no power but of God: the powers that be are ordained of God. Whosoever therefore resisteth the power, resisteth the ordinance of God: and they that resist shall receive to themselves damnation.
>
> [. . .]
>
> For this cause pay ye tribute also: for they are God's ministers, attending continually upon this very thing. Render to all what is due them: tax to whom tax is due; custom to whom custom; fear to whom fear; honor to whom honor.

With messages like these in mind, it is easy to see how difficult and important it was for Manegold of Lautenbach and Marsilius of Padua to take the steps they did in the Middle

Ages when they developed an independent theory of political legitimacy and dared drive a wedge between spiritual and secular power.

As Christianity grew in the Roman Empire, both church and state needed to make adjustments. Constantine saw the benefits of integrating this expanding faith and acknowledged its status as a religion in the early 300s. In turn, Christian leaders toned down the prohibition of manslaughter, which had been preventing Christians from serving in the imperial army. Later that century, Christianity was chosen as the empire's official religion.

As it continued to spread throughout Europe, Christianity was established from the top. This made religious leaders dependent on the secular rulers, but in turn, the church offered the state's reigning power structures its divine blessing, as well as literacy and administrative capabilities.

This unstable equilibrium between spiritual and secular power was disrupted during the High Medieval Period when Hildebrand, who was elected pope under the name of Gregory VII, challenged the imperial powers and demanded that the emperor bend his knee to the pope. In 1075, Hildebrand presented a reform program titled *Dictatus Papae*, which included twenty-seven brief statements on a new world order led by the pope and only the pope. According to the *Dictatus*, the pope would enjoy these privileges and more:

7. That to him alone is it permitted to make new laws according to the needs of the times.

9. That the pope alone is the one whose feet are to be kissed by all princes.

11. That he may depose emperors.

18. That no judgment of his may be revised by anyone, and that he alone may revise [the judgements] of all.

27. That he may absolve subjects of unjust men from [their oath] of fealty.

Neither party won a clear victory in this showdown, and when both the church's and the nobility's privileges were called into question across Europe a few centuries later, they united in defense of these privileges—a coalition that endures in modern times.

The Bible was used to validate existing power structures in a different way than *The Laws of Manu* were used in Hindu society. In contrast to Hinduism and Judaism (from which Christianity took the majority of its scriptures) Christianity has refrained from detailing how a society should be organized and governed. Even though the entire Torah was incorporated into the Bible, most of the commandments were disregarded and replaced with the New Testament's rather abstract and brief recommendations, along with the in-blank letter to the secular powers in Romans quoted above.

The Bible could however be used in more specific contexts. The Old Testament is a heterogeneous text, which is unsurprising considering that it was compiled over such a long period of time. It was further enriched by non-Judaic sources; a shining example of this is The Song of Solomon, which was borrowed from the Sumerians. The texts that comprise the New Testament were later added to this corpus. Instead of formulating specific rules for everyday life, as in *The Laws of Manu*, the Bible offers a cornucopia of myths, commandments, and historical fragments, and most rulers could find passages that supported their positions. There are many contradictions within these texts, but internal consistency is not a requirement on sacred texts in general.

In this sense, the legitimation of slavery is a particularly interesting example. Slavery seems to fundamentally contradict the idea that God created man in his image—and it stands to reason that this should guarantee some level of equality between people. But on the contrary, select passages in the Bible have been used to justify slavery for centuries. The key text— usually referred to as *Noah's curse*—is a relatively dark passage from Genesis 9, which reads:

> And Noah began *to be* a husbandman, and he planted a vineyard: And he drank of the wine, and was drunken; and he was uncovered within his tent. And Ham, the father of Canaan, saw the nakedness of his father, and told his two brethren without. And Shem and Japheth took a garment, and laid *it* upon both their shoulders, and went backward, and covered the nakedness of their father; and their faces *were* backward, and they saw not their father's na-

kedness. And Noah awoke from his wine, and knew what his younger son had done unto him.

And he said, Cursed *be* Canaan; a servant of servants shall he be unto his brethren.

And he said, Blessed *be* the LORD God of Shem; and Canaan shall be his servant.

God shall enlarge Japheth, and he shall dwell in the tents of Shem; and Canaan shall be his servant.

A modern reader might find this story somewhat illogical. Noah gets drunk and falls asleep naked in his tent. His son Ham happens to see him in this not-quite-respectable state and tells his brethren what he has seen. After Noah has slept himself sober, he finds out what has happened. Noah then condemns his grandson Canaan—not his son Ham—to a life of slavery even though the person who seems to have committed an offense is Noah himself. It is also unclear why Canaan should be condemned to slavery for a crime that his father is said to have committed. Even more interesting than these contradictions, however, is what has been made of this tale.

Keeping the name "Canaan" in mind, one can easily imagine the story originating in a territorial conflict between the Israelites and the Canaanites. The Torah contains many descriptions of conflicts between the Israelite monarchy and the neighboring peoples as well as quite brutal prescriptions for how these conflicts should be handled—a tool for nation-building. The Book of Jubilees, also known as "The Little Genesis" and probably written in the second century BCE, recounts this story from Genesis, but adds a detailed history of how the world was divided between the sons of Noah, leaving Africa to Ham; this prefigures some of the themes that would later be exploited by racists and proponents of slavery, namely proliferation and differentiation.

Early Jewish commentators increasingly came to associate the figure of Ham with worse crimes than speaking of his father's nudity—sodomy, adultery, and even the castration of his father—as well as associating him with dark skin, which paved the way for racist interpretations. When Christianity appropriated the Torah and renamed it "The Old Testament," authoritative church fathers such as Origen, Augustine, and Ambrose of Milan associated Ham and his descendants with sin and slavery. Augustine maintained that slavery was a punishment for past sins, thereby diagnosing it as a self-confirming condition. Something odd, but not out of context considering the long history of anti-Semitism in Christianity, is the identification of Ham with the Jews who saw Christ naked on the cross—yet another example of how pliant these texts can be in the hands of skilled interpreters.

During the 1400s, when the Spanish and the Portuguese started to trade slaves on a larger scale, Noah's curse was used to justify the African slave trade. Around 1700, it was being used as a defense of slavery in America, and later, during the eighteenth and nineteenth centuries, it became a main component of the slavery doctrine.

Noah's curse was also used in the Middle Ages to legitimate the dominance of the nobility and the clergy over the
Third Estate, casting farmers in the roles of Ham and Canaan—yet another illustration of the malleability of religious
myths in an ideological context.

The relationship between an age-old legacy and legitimacy
is particularly important in the history of Christianity. Objectively speaking, it is difficult to see Christianity as a continuation of Judaism in the way that mainstream Christianity
claims. After all, Paul and the church fathers did away with
most of the Jewish legacy contained in the Torah. Not even
the Ten Commandments—the core of Jewish ethics—were
left untouched, even though the Master himself declared his
fidelity to the law: "For verily I say unto you, Till heaven and
earth pass, one jot or one tittle shall in no wise pass from the
law, till all be fulfilled." The second commandment, the prohibition against producing images of God, which is also found
in Chapter 20 of Exodus, was simply omitted, and the tenth
commandment was split in two to preserve the total number.
Depicting various incarnations of the Holy Trinity was clearly
a far-too-potent weapon in the battle for souls to be sacrificed
by early Christian leaders. The logical conclusion would have
been to acknowledge Christianity's genuinely new character
and to limit its core religious legacy to the Gospels, Paul's
letters, and the other writings found in the New Testament.
When Marcion suggested this in the early second century, he
was branded a heretic and excommunicated. The venerable age
of Judaism's legacy was clearly (and probably correctly) deemed

an invaluable asset to a church trying to secure dominance on the religious scene.

## Religious Foundations: Islam

Islam sits between the poles of Hinduism's detailed regulation of social life and Christianity's more abstract legitimation of reigning power structures, but it sits closer to the former. Unlike Christianity, Islam evolved from a powerful position and did not need to compromise with secular powers over the governance of society. Religion, state, and society were entwined from the start; together they created the Muslim nation (*umma*). The European distinction between state and society, usually associated with the sixteenth-century philosopher Jean Bodin, is inconceivable in orthodox Islam. The same goes for the separation of church and state, a distinction that church fathers such as Origen were careful to uphold, but that was later dismantled in pace with the growing hunger for worldly power among church leaders.

Because in Islam the social order is thought to be of divine origin, like everything else on earth, it needs no further legitimation. Otherworldly wisdom has been revealed to the people, and it is not for them to question its origins or to seek alternatives to the status quo. The authoritative source is of course the Koran and *sharia*, which derives from it. The notion that the law was dictated to the Prophet by the divine authority is key to legitimating this source. Orthodox Muslims claim that the entire message was imparted during the Prophet's lifetime. Modern researchers have challenged this idea and estimate that it took almost half a millennium for Islam to find its present shape.

There are many parallels between Islam and Hinduism, and al-Biruni, a Muslim scholar in the 1000s, deemed the Indian caste system a model social hierarchy. But the two religions assert their legitimacy in different ways. In Islam, the Koran is the foundation of social order, and its importance stems from having found its definitive form at a certain point in history. Hinduism's closest equivalent is *The Laws of Manu*, but the Hindu doctrine tends to underscore the prehistoric tradition behind the text. Typically, modern introductions to Hinduism mention *Manu* only in passing, referring instead to the religion's long evolution: "There can be no doubt that the origins of Hinduism go back to a very distant past."

Whatever basis for legitimacy is asserted, society changes constantly, and situations that were not addressed in the religious records must be dealt with in some way. In a theocracy, the religious elite tries to have the sole right to adapt the framework as needed.

According to the Islamic world view, a social hierarchy is a prerequisite for order and is a natural result of the division of labor in a society:

> Do they distribute the mercy of your Lord? It
> is We who have apportioned among them their
> livelihood in the life of this world and have

raised some of them above others in degrees [of rank] that they may make use of one another for service. But the mercy of your Lord is better than whatever they accumulate.

That is the bounty of Allah, which He gives to whom He wills, and Allah is the possessor of great bounty.

To the extent that divine intervention is needed, it is argued that people are too equal to ever submit to anyone else of their own accord. It is through divine intervention that certain people are elevated above others and entrusted with the prerequisite authority.

After the first Muslim civil war, which shortly followed the Prophet's death and led to the establishment of *sunni* and *shia* factions, the concept of Islamic unity could no longer be upheld, neither on the religious nor on the political field. Muslim thinkers were forced to contemplate the same question of legitimacy that their European counterparts wrestled with during the Middle Ages. Should the head of state still be seen as a religious leader? How should one proceed if several leaders are fighting for power? Is it legitimate to oust a tyrant? No public conclusions were drawn. Citing general interest along with the proverb "The voice of the people is the voice of God" was not a solution in Islam, where society is believed to be ruled by a god, rather than by the people.

As for slavery, the litmus test of a moral system, the Koran, like its contemporary Christian sources, seems to take it as a given. Basically, Islamic law only allowed non-Muslims to be enslaved, and this was thought to be legitimate because slavery would give non-Muslims the chance to convert to the correct faith. This restriction has rarely been enforced. References to Noah's curse and the connection between skin color and slavery appear early on in Islamic literature, as do arguments against slavery, so the picture is mixed.

Historically speaking, the Muslim slave trade does not seem to have been any less extensive or less brutal than its European counterpart. The slave trade was preserved much longer in the Muslim world. When slavery finally became morally untenable in the West and in Russia around the mid-nineteenth century, the slave trade continued to be conducted mainly (but not exclusively) in Arab nations. International efforts to abolish slavery increased during the First World War, but they were met with strong resistance in the Muslim world. One particular challenge was the slave trade's relationship with the pilgrimage to Mecca (*hajj*). In Saudi Arabia, the annual prices for slaves peaked during *hajj*. Large crowds of (often young) pilgrims were encouraged to make this journey, often accompanied by a mentor, but upon arrival at this religious center, they were sold as slaves instead.

The Islamic republic of Mauritania finally outlawed slavery in the 1980s, which was something of a surprise. Slavery had officially been abolished in the country in 1905, when it was a French colony. But that ruling, based on a Western model of basic human rights, seemed half-hearted since *sharia* law took precedence when the constitution and Muslim law conflicted. *Sharia* courts put the slave-owners' rights before the slaves' when the new law was being tested. Slavery was still considered a social problem in Mauritania as recently as 1999, and as we move into the twenty-first century, the situation remains unclear. This problem also arose in other places, for example in the Republic of Sudan in the mid-1980s.

## Secular Foundations

Even though the religious solution to the legitimation problem has historically been by far the most important, the Enlightenment forced conservatives to present new arguments. For David Hume, the status quo was the obvious solution to the political problem. In *A Treatise on Human Nature*, he made the following argument about the distribution of property among citizens in a society:

> [. . .] it must immediately occur to them, as the most natural expedient, that every one continue to enjoy what he is at present master of, and that property or constant possession be conjoined to the immediate possession. Such is the effect of custom, that it not only reconciles us to any thing we have long enjoyed, but even gives us an affection for it, and makes us prefer it to other objects, which may be more valuable,

but are less known to us. What has long lain under our eye, and has often been employed to our advantage, that we are always the most un-willing to part with; but can easily live without possessions, which we never have enjoyed, and are not accustomed to. It is evident, therefore, that men would easily acquiesce in this expedi-ent, that every one continue to enjoy what he is at present possessed of; and this is the reason, why they would so naturally agree in prefer-ring it.

History has not validated Hume's optimistic hypothesis about a general acceptance of the status quo. Brian Barry has ad-dressed some of the problems with Hume's theory. First, it presumes that there is a status quo, which is not always the case; for instance, after a war or a decolonization. Even under less chaotic circumstances society will change; the tongue-in-cheek statement has been made that each generation of con-servatives will defend what their forefathers opposed. Going deeper, we find that references to the status quo become un-convincing as soon as citizens begin to question the founda-tions of this very status quo.

Otherwise, the standard conservative argument is that the very existence of a status quo proves that it is rational. As Jo-seph de Maistre wrote: "Custom is the mother of legitimacy." Burke asserted that custom was our "second nature," a thesis that would be oft repeated. In the absence of other arguments, it comes dangerously close to Dr. Pangloss's assertion—that we live in a world in which everything is ordered in the best possible way, for if it was not the best, it would not be ordered in this way.

When history verges on myth, leaders often seek legitimacy by claiming they have descended in a direct lineage from the first inhabitants of the territory. This is why the official version of South African history during the apartheid period claimed that the country was empty before the arrival of its inhabitants around 1600, and archeological findings that predated that arrival literally were hidden away in archeology departments in South African universities. The boundary is not clear; in the Middle East, arguments like these are entwined with religious or pseudo-religious arguments.

If we carefully add an evolutionary perspective to the concept of the status quo, then society could be seen as a system of rules that is continually adjusted in light of experience and thereby preserves the rationality of the system. In this configuration, conservatism seems more like liberalism, and it is often hard to separate the views of conservative liberals like von Hayek from this version of conservatism. The analogy with biological evolution is risky, and organic theories are usually looked upon with skepticism by more modern conservatives.

Somewhat surprisingly, de Maistre, the firmly anti-liberal conservative philosopher, makes a utilitarian argument in one of his works, and it sounds bewilderingly like Jeremy Bentham: "The best government for each nation is that which, in the territory occupied by this nation, is capable of producing the greatest possible sum of happiness and strength, for the greatest possible number of men, during the longest possible time." An argument like this is rare among conservatives for the simple reason that it is extremely difficult to derive the status quo from a formula this abstract. Furthermore, this statement does not lead to a mathematically meaningful problem, so even in the best of all worlds, there is no solution.

## The Redistribution of Income and Wealth

In spite of this generally fragmented picture of conservatism, attitudes toward the redistribution of income and wealth are more predictably homogeneous. Conservative thought, whether it has a religious or a secular foundation, does not question spontaneous redistribution in a society. Solidarity with the weak is part of Christianity, and alms-giving is one of Islam's five pillars. In the same way, modern secular conservatism advocates voluntary contributions and will even consider using state subsidies funded by taxes for such contributions, which might seem contradictory. What is not acceptable is for the state to be used as an instrument of redistribution to the extent that it upsets the balance of economic power.

One basis for conservatism's attitude to redistribution is knowledge skepticism, both generally and regarding social processes. Because our knowledge of these processes is limited at best, we take a significant risk when we try to influence them in some essential way. Here, conservative thought intersects with Robert Merton's previously mentioned tenet on the unintended consequences of human actions. Behavioral patterns that are rational on a small scale sometimes lead to unforeseen consequences when combined on a social level. These surprises might yield positive or negative results, but conservative writers tend to focus on the latter when they discuss active intervention. Two examples are price regulation and the minimum wage, which are said to harm the groups they are meant to help.

Such arguments gain strength when the unintended consequences are said to threaten central functions and institutions in society. Thinkers including William Mallock and Friedrich von Hayek have argued for the positive value of inequality in society and have pointed out the risks taken when trying to increase equality, similar to the Humboldtian argument cited in the previous chapter.

As a natural consequence of knowledge skepticism, conservatism is inherently critical of theories about the social contract, whichever conclusions can be drawn from such approaches. The idea that it is in some way possible to reconstruct social institutions from a pure state of nature or from the contract theorists' starting point goes against conservatism's world view. Thus, an attempt is made to deprive egalitarian theories of one of their chief instruments for formulating an alternative to the status quo.

A different but important aspect of conservatism is its general attitude to moral relativism and national character. It was from a context like this that the German Counter-

Enlightenment movement was born around 1800, a movement in direct opposition to Enlightenment philosophers' efforts to establish universal values for humanity and a scientific standard independent of the cultural climate. These relativist attitudes give rise to further arguments against implementing distribution policies in social contexts or, in more ideological terms, against the right to use egalitarian values as a starting point for a political discussion in a society where they are not embraced by all.

In reality, something other than knowledge skepticism and concern about difference lies behind the conservative attitude toward active intervention. The crucial observation is that in a society, the state is the only institution that can balance out the private exercise of power that is connected to economic resources. The main (and logical) goal of the politics of the right is to weaken government, chiefly through limiting taxes and increasing the scope for the private exercise of power. These politics have become most pronounced in the United States, where the right's campaign against the state in recent decades has taken on nearly religious undertones.

# 9

## SOCIAL DEMOCRACY AND INEQUALITY

*The problem with social democracy—which retains
the market as an institution—is finding the right
balance between the economic and political spheres
and keeping that balance once it has been found.*

As we saw in the historical overview at the start of the book,
humankind has a long tradition of thinking of inequality as a
problem and exploring how it can be managed. It is addressed
in Sumerian and Egyptian texts, the Jewish Book of Jubilees,
the reforms of Solon in Athens, the peasant revolts during the
Middle Ages, and later. But it was during the Enlightenment
that the tradition first began to develop a theoretical platform
for the analysis and reformation of social structures. Industri-
alization, literacy, and the growth of social strata not bound by
loyalty to the old regime cleared the path for a broad questioning of how society had hitherto been organized.

Quite early on in this process, clear-thinking observers

realized that universal suffrage was the logical end point of development. The leaders of the old regime did their best to delay it, but they could not prevent it. To a degree, the level of their resistance was determined by what they felt their odds were, using the new playbook, of getting through this transition with their power intact.

Liberals and socialists agreed on the basic constitutional question of universal suffrage, but within the left there was doubt as to how sufficient the framework of constitutional democracy was in the fight for social and economic equality. Eventually, the left split into a social-democratic branch, which thought it was sufficient, and a communist branch, which had other ideas. Essentially, communists did not assume that legislation could ever exert sufficient control over the national economy, and so believed that the majority of economic resources should be publicly owned. As twentieth-century history showed, communist regimes were not satisfied with controlling the most important means of production; they also took over mass media, culture, and other building blocks of what is usually called civil society.

## The Absence of a Stable, Egalitarian Equilibrium

The conclusion that there is no stable, egalitarian equilibrium in the bargaining game can be taken as a point strongly in favor of left-wing ideologies. The implication is that there is no neutral ground-state in the economic arena, but that instead it is inevitably characterized by an ongoing fight between rival groups, constantly changing coalitions, and shifts in the balance of power. It is here that social democrats and left liberals differ most clearly: the latter are likely to assume that the market and democracy generate real competitive behaviors and a tolerant political environment. This is clearly not the case. In the economic sphere, special-interest groups are always working to forward their own agendas, and in the absence of corrective measures, they will not hesitate to undermine the mechanisms needed for the market to function, as Adam Smith already observed:

> People of the same trade seldom meet together, even for merriment and diversion, but the conversation ends in a conspiracy against the publick, or in some contrivance to raise prices. It is impossible indeed to prevent such meetings, by any law which either could be executed, or would be consistent with liberty and justice. But though the law cannot hinder people of the same trade from sometimes assembling together, it ought to do nothing to facilitate such assemblies; much less to render them necessary.

In this endless bid for more power, larger companies will have more influence than smaller ones and larger trade organizations will be more successful than smaller ones. Successful organizations tend to grow, which leads to the positive feedback that gives rise to instability.

The idea that there is only one equilibrium in the bargaining game and that it is unstable is a strong argument for state intervention in general. This means that political intervention in the players' negotiations is necessary if you want to keep one player from eventually exploiting the other. It is more a question of *when* the state's powers should come into play than *if* they should. This does not only apply to the night-watchman state—administration of justice, defense, and other core functions of the state—a point on which most writers agree. It definitely pertains to questions of distribution as well. Of course there will not be a consensus on what constitutes a reasonable level of ambition, but the qualitative conclusion should be clear to all participants in the political debate, whatever their ideological affiliation.

At first glance, the role that chance plays in who gets the upper hand in a negotiation also speaks strongly in favor of left-wing ideologies. If three main factors determine success—chance, inheritance, and effort—and the first two are dominant, then the legitimacy of the reigning power structure is threatened in societies in which the state does not correct spontaneous outcomes. Even if efforts are not unimportant to the direction that development will take, over time the self-reinforcing mechanism in negotiations will lead to results that are not at all proportionate to variances in effort.

But the inherent instability in the balance of power is also a problem for a society equipped with a strong state. This is because it is only in abstract models that democratic decisions are made in the public square, the *agora*, after thorough debate based on rational arguments. In reality, a division of labor occurs in all democracies between those in power and the voters, also when social democrats are in control. Direct democracy as it is practiced in Switzerland and in sporadic referendums in representative democracies does not solve this problem and is not a model that should be emulated.

Whichever decision-making process one employs to manage the surplus in a society with predominantly state ownership, certain groups will have greater influence than others, and they will in all likelihood use their influence to strengthen their own positions. In communist societies, the division of labor is even more pronounced. The ruling elite are always better informed about the country's administration than the population at large and can use this knowledge to their advantage. The inherent instability in negotiation afflicts also communist societies, as twentieth-century history makes painfully clear. The risk for a concentration of power is higher in a communist economy than in a market economy, because the latter does in fact have the potential for innovation and challenge of existing cartels.

This is the main point at which social democracy and communism diverge. Social democracy draws an adequate conclusion from the basic dilemma and uses the state as a mechanism to control the fundamental instability in negotiations. Communism makes the state party to the conflict in its attempt to eliminate difference once and for all. And by outlawing private ownership, at least on a social level, it hopes to eliminate other groups competing for power in society. But even in a society like this, negotiations are a source of instability and, as such, of inequality, regardless of which institutions one establishes to manage the surplus, so the conflict will end up being imported into the political realm.

The problem that social democracy, which retains the market as an institution, has is finding the right balance between the economic and political spheres and keeping that balance once it has been found. Although social democracy and communism analyze a market-based society's inherent oppositions and conflicts in a similar fashion, they arrive at completely different conclusions when it comes to practical politics—not unlike the Rhine and the Donau. The two rivers' sources are near each other in Central Europe, but they flow in very different directions, one ending in the North Sea and the other in the Black.

## Redistribution Strategies

Social democracy's big trade-off dilemma concerns the level of ambition considered reasonable when building a more equal society and choosing the best measures for implementing this project. If you start from a pure market solution, measures that aim to increase equality often go hand in hand with an increased rate of economic growth, but at a certain (unknown) point, an increase in equality is likely only to be achieved at the expense of the labor supply and savings, and there has to be a trade-off.

A traditional social-democratic strategy builds on a wide spectrum of measures that level out both conditions and results. The most important instrument in the former is an active education policy targeting social groups who historically have a low level of participation in education. These policies have been successful to an extent. Postwar education reform resulted in improved long-term salary trends for children from working-class backgrounds. Another important measure of success in equalizing the conditions related to income is the difference in income between parents and their children. If the correlation is strong, then one can assume that children do not have equal opportunities, and there is reason to believe that equalization would simultaneously reduce this gap and increase the potential for growth. The Nordic countries fare better than the United States over this matter; in the Nordic countries, the correlation between parents' and children's income is weaker than in the United States. Furthermore, the correlation between siblings' income is stronger in the latter country, which is also an indication that family background is a more important factor there. An active education policy seems to be a requirement if the liberal idea of establishing relatively equal conditions for the younger generation is to be realized.

The second key component to a social-democratic strategy is a well-developed social security system. This system has the two-pronged effect of transmitting resources from middle and high earners to those with a low income and strengthening the position of employees in relation to the holders of capital. The first effect occurs because low income earners benefit more from the social security system (for example, their sick-leave absence is higher), and yet the contributions to the system are not based on risk. In a market-based system, premiums would be set in relation to risk, and no transfer would take place. This transfer is significant—more so, in fact, than the effect of central government income tax in Sweden.

The indirect effect of a social security system (strengthening workers' positions in negotiations about the terms of employment) is hard to quantify, but it is most likely greater than the direct effect. One reason that assessing the effect is so difficult is that countries with well-developed social security systems also tend to have relatively strong trade unions, which work toward a similar end.

Taxation is the third important factor in social-democratic leveling-out policies. The combined effect of the tax-and-transfer system is influenced by a number of factors, and the profile of income- and wealth-tax systems is only one of them. A proportional tax that finances a public service consumed equally by everyone has a leveling effect, so there is no radical qualitative difference between proportional and progressive taxes.

Taking their cue from the United States and beginning in the 1980s, various OECD countries have moved toward establishing a wider tax base, lower tax rates, and less progressive tax scales. In recent years, both inheritance tax and wealth tax have been done away with in Sweden, and real-estate tax has been drastically decreased. Behind this movement is allegedly a growing worry about the cost of equality policies. Arthur Okun summarized this trade-off problem in his oft-quoted book *Equality and Efficiency: The Big Tradeoff*. He uses a leaking bucket as a metaphor for the problem; the government wants to equalize income by transferring resources from the better-off to the worse-off, but resources get lost along the way. So what is a reasonable trade-off?

A few words of warning. Okun's metaphor can be interpreted as meaning that all policies that level out differences have costs, or inversely that an increase in income inequality automatically leads to a higher rate of economic growth. But neither is the case. Education policies have reduced differences in both conditions and outcomes, and these changes can be expected to lead to attainment of careers being increasingly based on merit and less on family background. The connection between equality and economic development is complicated.

There is also no simple correlation between public spending and the long-term growth rate, and there are several reasons why there cannot be. To begin with, differences in how countries administrate their tax-and-transfer systems impact the size of their public sector. Resources can be transferred through tax deductions, such as tax-free donations or introducing transfers alongside income tax. In Sweden, it was not long ago that there were tax scales based on family status, but in the current tax system, such elements have been done away with. Child benefit is a prime example of an untaxed transfer, but generally transfers are taxed in a social security system.

These three basic solutions—deductions, untaxed transfers, and taxed transfers, respectively—may yield the same result for households, but their impact on both public-sector size and total taxation is completely different. It is estimated that the American welfare sector would be approximately 50 percent larger if the second administrative solution was employed. For this reason, the public sector in Scandinavian countries looks larger than it actually is. The deviation that occurs when comparing otherwise quite similar OECD countries is systematic; in countries with a strong political tradition of criticizing the government, like the United States, politicians show a clear preference for solutions that make government seem smaller.

More important, public spending impacts households and the national economy in completely different ways, depending on where the money goes. Certain expenditures—for example, public funds spent on culture—have limited direct effects on the economy, but subsidized childcare has a direct positive impact on the labor supply. In the same way, certain taxes can be expected to have a greater effect on behavior than others. With this in mind, it is hardly surprising that economists arrive at different conclusions about the effects of the level of public spending on the economic growth rate; some have found negative effects to be negative, others positive, but the majority seem unsure of the consequences.

On a micro-level—taking the household's perspective— the effects of the social security system are documented. The rules that govern unemployment insurance, health insurance, and pensions impact how actively people look for work, the number of sick days taken, and retirement plans. The effects are as expected: generous systems lead to a smaller labor supply, although the effects in some cases are small and in some cases statistically insignificant. In the same way, there is evidence of the indirect costs of taxation, even if the size of the effect is highly uncertain.

To summarize, every overly ambitious distribution policy has its costs, and those costs tend to increase more than proportionally in relation to ambition once a certain level is exceeded. So, the question of what a reasonable level of ambition is remains unanswered; the answer depends on political priorities. Table 3.1 in Chapter 3 shows significant variances among OECD countries in the distribution of disposable income—variances that specifically reflect different political priorities.

The conclusion that inequality cannot completely be eliminated may be hard to swallow for many leftists. But perhaps the idea of a perfect egalitarian society is more a feature of political rhetoric than a serious political objective.

## Why Engage?

For the conservative skeptic, the social-democratic bid for equality is no different from any other impulse born of self-interest. Each social class tends to its own interests, and one movement is not morally superior to another. At the same time, these very skeptics should ask themselves why so many people throughout history have gotten involved in an issue that clearly does not benefit them personally. The Egyptian bureaucrat quoted in the first chapter was not a poor man speaking for himself. And yet he was so strongly disposed to make his deeds known that he let them be inscribed on his tomb. What lies behind this impulse?

If you turn the question over to Frans de Waal, the primatologist cited in Chapter 3, he would say that we are compassionate by nature. In a book tellingly called *Good Natured*, he argues that the moral reflex predates our species. People can of course develop other behavioral patterns—indifference, recklessness, even brutality—but compassion is also an option and can become the norm under the right circumstances.

There is another, more modern answer to the question that might speak to those who want a reason more concrete than human nature to support the idea of a highly egalitarian society. This answer is connected to modern social-science research into trust and social capital and the consequences of the trust level being high or low. Trust can be measured in different ways; either you ask people if they trust their neighbors, politicians, and others whom they encounter in their everyday lives, or you measure the strength of a civil society by the level of involvement in organizations and other voluntary activities. It turns out that it does not much matter which method you choose; the results will be similar.

A consistent observation is that trust and equality have a strong correlation: the more equal a society is, the more trust the people in that society feel toward each other. Diagram 9.1

here shows the connection between the Gini coefficient and the degree of trust, measured in seventy-five countries. The correlation has been verified by a number of researchers using different methods and can be considered reliable. Note the exceptionally high level of trust and equality in the Nordic countries.

The second step in the argument is that societies with a high degree of trust generally function better. The American political scientist Robert Putnam has systematically investigated the prerequisites of trust and its consequences. The fifty United States of America provide fertile ground for comparison because their histories are so varied—different patterns of immigration, slavery in the South, and so on. It turns out

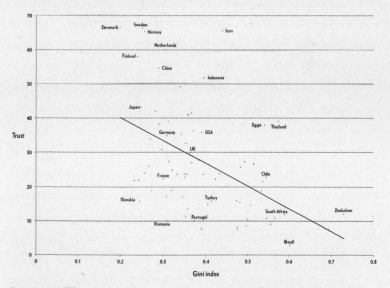

Diagram 9.1. The connection between difference in income (measured with the Gini coefficient) and the level of trust in seventy-five societies: the higher the disparity in income, the lower the trust. The correlation is −0.47. The data are from the middle and later part of the 1990s. (Source: Jordahl [2009])

that the single factor that creates the surest basis for predicting the level of trust in a state is the percentage of the population that descended from Scandinavian immigrants. But
it gets even more interesting when connections are made between the measured trust level and various objective measures
of the state of a society. Here are a few of Putnam's findings:

+ In states with high trust, the schools function better, however the results are measured.
+ In states with high trust, children and youths fare
  better, measured in infant mortality, teen preg-
  nancy, and other health variables.
+ In states with high trust, the rate of violent crime
  is lower.
+ In states with a strong sense of solidarity, people
  are generally healthier.
+ States with high trust have lower levels of tax eva-
  sion, as estimated by the American Internal Revenue Service.

The strength of these observations varies. An international
debate, connected to Richard Wilkinson's *The Impact of Inequality*, is ongoing about the connection between health and
equality, and one could say that the question is still on the
table. Most investigations into the connection between trust
and the economic growth rate suggest a rather strong positive
connection.

Causation can go in either direction; societies can get into positive or negative spirals as trust rises or falls. But Putnam's conclusions paint a coherent picture that seems highly plausible.

The conclusion here is not that the level of trust in a society can be increased quickly and easily by expanding the tax and transfer systems. Trust and equality are multi-dimensional, and a long-term strategy for strengthening them must address a number of relevant areas—education, health, disposable income, and more.

Beyond the discussions about human nature and the importance of trust is another aspect that should also be of interest to those who accept only economic arguments: equality of opportunity is conducive to growth. The World Bank in its *World Development Report 2006* summarized the experience from a number of countries that had made the journey from the low- to middle-income category starting in 1960. The question asked was what the impact was of the distribution of assets at the starting point on the rate of growth during the four decades that followed. Given that these countries were all agricultural economies at the outset, it was the distribution of arable land that was of importance. The conclusion from the analysis was very clear: the countries that had the most even distribution of land in 1960 were also the ones that had the highest growth during the four decades that followed.

In developed industrial countries, education rather than land is the key asset. For such countries, Miles Corak has established an equally clear connection between income distribution and mobility, nick-named "the Great Gatsby curve." Income mobility is considered a good indicator of how well a society rewards ability before family background. Mobility is measured using the correlation between parents' income and that of their children when grown-ups; the stronger the correlation, the lower the mobility. Also in this context there is a clear pattern; countries that have the most unequal distribution of incomes are also the ones that exhibit the lowest mobility, as illustrated in Diagram 9.2 below.

We are back where we started, with the two boys playing marbles. If the distribution of the marbles is skewed when the game starts, the risk is high that the best player does not win.

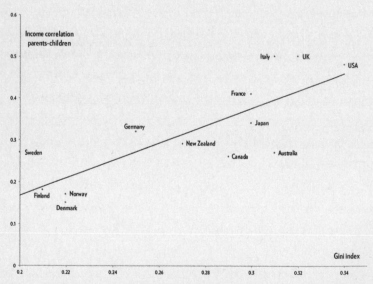

Diagram 9.2. The "Great Gatsby curve": connection between income distribution and income mobility. Along the horizontal axis is measured the Gini index of disposable income in 1985; along the vertical, the correlation between parents' income and that of their children when grown-ups toward the end of the 1990s. The children in the study were born in the 1960s. The more unequal the income distribution, the more children's incomes depend on those of their parents. (Source: Corak [2013])

The general conclusion is worth considering, even for the skeptic: a more egalitarian society might be the better option even for those who do not derive direct or short-term benefits from such a change.

## What Is to Be Done?

The reason why policies of redistribution in the Nordic countries during the twentieth century were successful is that a broad spectrum of instruments were used—education, labor market policy, social insurance, taxes, and transfers. The discussion around the work of Thomas Piketty and his colleagues has been dominated by the issue of capital taxation, which is too narrow a perspective. Certain of the above instruments have become more difficult to use as a result of globalization, whereas national governments retain full authority over education and labor market policy. If political goals remain the same, the natural response to globalization would be to work more intensively with the instruments over which one still has control. In that perspective, the steadily decreasing quality of the system of education and the erosion of labor market norms are serious. Further, the possibilities of taxing international capital appear greater than has hitherto been claimed. In the aftermath of the latest financial crisis, there is increased political pressure for greater transparency in tax havens such as Switzerland, Luxemburg, and some island nations, for international registers of beneficial owners, and for standards for the taxation of transnational corporations. Coordination in the area of international taxation seems to have been blocked less by technical problems than by political lack of interest.

The conclusion is that the varied tool box used in the postwar period for developing the Nordic welfare states has not lost its relevance. The important insight to be gained is that the problem of keeping inequality at a reasonable level cannot be solved by any single measure but requires broad spectrum of measures that aim at both equalizing opportunities for individuals to shape their own lives and at equalizing outcomes such as disposable income.

# 10

## CLOSING THE BOOK

*A society is not an inanimate object;*
*it is a human artifact.*

Three questions were posed at the start of the book. The first was "Why are all societies unequal?" As we have seen, inequality between individuals and groups is not what needs to be explained; it is a direct result of the human constitution—how we experience the world around us and how we relate to risk—combined with how bargaining games and markets tend to develop under general conditions. Small differences in basic conditions—differences that do not necessarily have anything to do with talent or effort—will intensify over time and grow without limit. The only limit to the stronger player's action is that player's interest in keeping the other player alive so that society can continue to exist.

This is not to say that there are no differences in talent or effort, only that these do not even come close to explaining the disparity we see in income and assets. So, the wrong question is being asked. Equality—not inequality—is what needs to be explained. Why do some societies succeed in upholding a decent level of equality in spite of the natural tendency to move toward the inequality limit?

The second question was "Can inequality be influenced?" The answer is in the affirmative. We are not fated to live with inequality. Indeed, unregulated negotiation processes are unstable and will exacerbate difference, but these processes can be managed. Engineers know how to control instability and can even build it into their designs. One look at the Gini coefficient for income or assets in OECD countries, which are economically and socially similar, reveals great disparities between the countries—disparities that are political in origin.

The third question was "How do the classical ideologies relate to inequality as a phenomenon?" Liberalism has often underscored the importance of having similar points of departure in life so that genuine differences in talent and effort can come to the fore. At the same time, liberalism has underestimated the self-reinforcing mechanism—the main topic of this book—and so it falls embarrassingly silent in the discussion about what should be done in practice about the vast differences in the social contexts into which people are born. Conservatism makes the same mistake, if it is even a mistake at all, and suffers from significant legitimacy problems when explanations and justifications are demanded for historical and present-day distributions of assets and income. Social democracy is the ideology that comes out best in light of the perspectives explored and the conclusions that have been drawn. You could say that among these three ideological alternatives, it is social democracy that has taken the liberal demand for a level playing field the most seriously. And yet, social democracy has historically struggled with deciding how far to take its bid for equality and with finding the correct methods for realizing its ambitions. This is not surprising; it is a genuinely difficult problem.

The diagram of the inequality limit in Chapter 3 (Diagram 3.2) shows that for every level of economic development there are an upper and a lower limit of equality in society—total equality relative to the inequality possibility frontier, where the latter is equivalent to a small group controlling the entire surplus while most of the rest of the population lives at the subsistence level. A society's distance from the inequality frontier is a measure of how civil it is.

Without an active distribution policy, society moves as relentlessly toward the inequality limit as a stone plummets to the ground when dropped, falling with each moment that passes unless it encounters some resistance. But a society is not an inanimate object; it is a human artifact. With the right design and vigilant policies, it can be kept in the air as successfully as the Wright brothers' flying machine.

Inequality is part of the human condition, but it can be influenced. As this discussion has shown, staving off a spontaneous and unjustifiably high level of inequality is a Sisyphean task. But following Camus we must imagine Sisyphus happy in his endeavors.

# NOTES

If no other source is cited, all quotations are translated by Saskia Vogel.

v **"It is the common fate":** The quotation is taken from John Philpot Curran: "Election of Lord Mayor of Dublin," speech before the Privy Council, in Dublin 1790 (Curran 1865, p. 105).

## Chapter 1: Inequality and Its Shadow

3 *"Who knows the orphan"* and *"I was collected":* The Sumerian quotation (first) is taken from Kramer (1981), p. 104, and the Egyptian one from Parkinson (1991), p. 63.
General references to the background of the history of ideas are Sabine & Thorson (1973), Strauss & Cropsey (eds.) (1987), and Kymlicka (1990).

7 **Although the idea of a social contract lost some of its appeal:** Rawls (1972), Nozick (1974).

## Chapter 2: Playing Marbles

11  **The British organization Oxfam:** Oxfam (2015).

12  ***"On the square one day":*** Sten Selander's poem is taken from his collection *Staden and andra dikter* (*The City and Other Poems*) (1926).

14  **To attain an answer:** The analysis of the random walk using Markov chains was conducted in Kemeny & Snell (1976).

16  **Success in competition:** Dr. Pangloss is a character in Voltaire's *Candide* (1759). I wrote an article about the Pangloss paradigm in *Tvärsnitt* (*Cross Section*) (1984), which also references further literature that questions the rationality of evolution.

**"Does the fittest necessarily survive?":** Shubik's analysis of the duel is found in Shubik (1954).

17  **We often assume that the Panglossian idea:** On sexual reproduction, see Emlen & Oring (1977); on elephant seals specifically, Le Boeuf (1974).

18  **Certain thinkers have even wanted to posit exchange as a social equivalent to chemical bonds:** For general information on exchange theory, see Bredemeier (1978), Coleman (1990), Homans (1961).

19  **Such negotiation games:** Practical illustrations of the bargaining problem can also be found in Fisher & Ury (1981) and Raiffa (1982).

**Tourists who haggle at a bazaar in a foreign country might enjoy the process itself:** Models of political negotiation are a large and contentious field of research. Mueller (1989) and Ordeshook (1992) contain overviews of the literature that build on economic models of rationality; examples include Downs (1957), Buchanan & Tullock (1962), and Buchanan

(1975). Critical analyses of the theory using political science as a starting point can be found in Barry (1965), and using sociology in Udehn (1996).

21 **"This division of labour":** The Adam Smith quotation is taken from *The Wealth of Nations*, Book I, Ch. II.

22 **Negotiations have not been limited to exchanges of goods and services:** On bartered brides and wedding dowries, see Goody (1983).

   **Gift-giving is a form of exchange:** Classics named in the text are Durkheim (1893), Malinowski (1922), and Mauss (1923–1924).

## Chapter 3: The Archeology of Inequality

26 **It should be noted that even with the fairly detailed data available on industrialized countries today:** On measures of inequality, see Atkinson (1983) and Cowell (2000).

   **But distribution is not only about income and resources:** The importance of analyses of inequality taking differences in opportunity into account and not just real assets has been highlighted by Amartya Sen; see Sen (1985, 1992).

28 **You might be wondering how literature on primate behavior is relevant to a discussion about equality:** For studies of primates, see de Waal (2005), Gallup (1970), Byrne & Whiten (1997), Goodall (1990).

30 **In contrast to chickens, which have a simple pecking order:** On pecking order among poultry, see Schjelderup-Ebbe (1922).

32 **Behavioral researchers have long discussed:** On the hypothesis of a dominance drive, see Maslow (1933–1934).

**"So that in the first place":** The Hobbes quotation is from *Leviathan*, Hobbes (1651), Ch. 11.

33 **Every reconstruction of prehistoric hunter-gatherer societies:** For a general overview, see Brown (1991), Scarr (ed.) (2005). See also Evans-Pritchard (1940), Sahlins (1972), Service (1975). On the development of social intelligence, see also Boehm (1997) and Barton & Dunbar (1997).

34 **Olga Soffer has given an account:** On the Central Russian plains, Soffer (1985).

35 **Per Lekberg offers a similar perspective:** Lekberg (2002).

36 **Farming presupposes settlement:** Bowles et al. (2010).
   **For hunter-gatherer societies:** Smith et al. (2010).
   *Horticultural societies:* Gurven et al. (2010).

37 In *pastoral societies:* Borgerhoff Mulder et al. (2010).
   **In a general study of nearly 200 societies, slavery was shown to be rather common:** Murdock & White (2010).

38 **War was not unknown among hunter-gatherer societies:** Taçon & Chippendale (1994).
   **Organized resistance against such raids:** The importance of the production of organized violence to the social structure is explored by Boix (2010).

39 **the classic trio of plough, sword, and book:** Gellner (1988). On irrigation systems, see Wittfogel (1957); critical analyses can be found in Butzer (1976) and Mann (1986).
   **Using the same measuring techniques:** Gini coefficients for agricultural societies have been computed by Shenk et al. (2010).

40 **Material resources are now the most important factor:** On transmission between generations in various societies, see Smith et al. (2010).

NOTES                                                                189

41 **Through the historiography that developed in Greece and Rome:** On the distribution of assets in Athens, see Foxhall (2002) and Osborne (1992), quoted in Scheidel (2010).

**But of course, democratic Athens had its blemishes:** Classical analyses of Athens's social structure are found in Burns (1966) and Finley (1953).

**The Athens of the 500s played host:** A thorough analysis of the reforms of Solon based on contemporary documents appears in Stanton (1990).

42 **The Gini coefficient for income distribution in classical Rome:** Milanović et al. (2007).

43 **Famine, as best we know, was uncommon in ancient Greece and Rome:** Garnsey (1988).

44 **A few general observations:** An overview of the economic and demographic history of the last 1,000 years is found in Maddison (2001).

45 **A selection of point estimates:** For England: Bekar & Reed (2009) and Campbell (2008); for Paris: Sussmann (2008); for Byzantium and Rome: Milanović (2006) and Milanović et al. (2007), respectively.

46 **Slavery was widespread in Europe:** On the development of the trans-oceanic slave trade, see Thomas (1997).

**With the dawn of the new era:** Lindert (2000), Soltow & van der Zanden (1998) and Morrison (2000).

47 **Even though the richer OECD countries:** OECD (2011) contains and overview of development in OECD countries in recent decades. See also Brandolini & Smeeding (2009) and Immervoll & Richardson (2011).

50 **Worldwide, the disparities are even greater:** Ferreira & Ravallion (2009).

This connection is complex, and the relationship between growth and income distribution can go either way: Voitchovsky (2009).

Over a longer time span: Bourguignon & Morrisson (2002).

51  Theoretical and Factual Inequality: This section is based on Milanović et al. (2007).

56  Sudden changes in the environment: The ability of those previously in power to weather the transition to Europe's new conditions is analyzed in Mayer (1981).

## Chapter 4: The End of the Tale

57  *"Sweet little child, the story ends here"*: Sigfrid Lindström's poem was first published in the 1927 collection *De besegrade* (*The Vanquished*).

62  Bargaining According to Nash: Nash's Ph.D. thesis (Nash 1950) and a number of other key texts are found in Kuhn & Nasar (2002). For a modern account, see, for example, Osborne & Rubinstein (1990).

64  There is empirical evidence for the law's application: Dehaene (2003).

65  In the decades since Nash presented his work: An overview of developments since Nash's initial contribution with key publications by other researchers is found in Thomson (ed.) (2010). The main alternatives to Nash's bargaining solution are the Kalai-Smorodinsky's solution (Kalai & Smorodinsky 1975) and the so-called egalitarian bargaining solution (Kalai 1977) (which isn't particularly egalitarian). Ok (1998) has shown that Nash's solution represents an effective balance between efficiency and distributive aims, while Kalai-

Smorodinsky's solution doesn't. Nash's theory is similar to the one Kenneth Arrow was using at the same time to analyze collective decision-making problems; see Arrow (1950), Kelly (1978).

Nash proposed a strategic model that renders the bidding process as an alternative to his main model. More realistic models had already been developed by Zeuthen (1930), and one was later presented by Harsanyi (1956). Currently, the model that is most used is from Ståhl (1972) and Rubinstein (1982); see also Ståhl (1994). Further arguments for Nash's solution are found in van Damme (1986) and Young (1993).

67 **The Long-term Dynamic of the Bargaining Game:** The proof for the claim doesn't require anything more advanced than freshman mathematics at a university level (derivatives and integrals). The attitude towards risk is defined with the help of Arrow-Pratt's measures of risk aversion (Pratt 1964; Arrow 1965, 1971). The requirement that the attitude towards risk decrease in pace with an increase in assets is necessary. For a discussion of empirical data around this requirement, see Meyer & Meyer (2006). The proof can be presented on request.

71 **"What are the common wages of labour":** The quotation is from Smith's *The Wealth of Nations* and is taken from Book I, Ch. VIII.

72 **So far, the analysis has been limited:** Fernholz and Fernholz (2014).

75 **The Bridge Between *Is* and *Ought*:** Hume's discussion of the relationship between *ought* and *is* is found in Hume (1739–1740), Book III, Part I, Section I. Hume's thesis was further developed by Moore (1903), Hägerström (1911); for a critical analysis see Prior (1960) and Searle (1964).

**Modern research into logic has confirmed this conclusion:** Schurz (1997).

## Chapter 5: The Art of Flying

77 **On December 17, 1903:** A good account of the attempts to fly with machines that were heavier than air is found in Tobin (2003).

78 **"It was nevertheless the first time":** The quotation from Orville Wright is in Wright (1913).

**This event had enormous implications:** For more on the connection between the development of transport technology and the spread of contagious diseases, see McNeill (1976).

82 **"Skill comes by":** The quotation from Wilbur Wright is taken from Jakab & Young (eds.) (2000).

**To relieve the pilot of this tiring task:** For more on Elmer Sperry's contributions, see Hughes (1971).

**Autopilots operate:** On ship steering: Källström (1979).

83 **Keynes once noted:** See Keynes (1936) on the intellectual dependency on deceased economists.

84 **Instability can arise spontaneously:** The origins of feedback control can be found in Mayr (1969). Early important contributions are collected in Bellman & Kalaba (1964).

**What moral statements are supposed to be about has long been debated in philosophy:** Frankena (1973), Mackie (1977).

85 **Taking an evolutionary view:** Ullman-Margalit (1977).

**Moral norms and other codes of conduct:** Standard references for moral maturity are Piaget (1932/1960) and Kohlberg (1981).

87 **In our second example:** On tithes, see Lane Fox (1986), Ch. 10.

**These are two historically significant examples:** Similar critical thoughts on the search for the perfect constitution are found in Sen (2009).

## Chapter 6: Back to the Social Contract

89 **"The other party":** The quotation is from Hume (1742). General references for the survey of the history of ideas is as mentioned above (Ch. 1): Sabine & Thorson (1973), Strauss & Cropsey (eds.) (1987) and Kymlicka (1990). For an overview more focused on the distribution problem as such, see Sandmo (2014).

91 **"*Nor did I deem*":** The quotation from Sophocles' *Antigone* is taken from E. H. Plumptre's translation.

94 **"Therefore since all men are free by nature":** The quotation from Nicholas of Cusa is from Nicholas of Cusa (2010).

95 **Robert Filmer, a royalist and later a target:** The Filmer quotation is from Filmer (1652).

96 **"The obligation of subjects to the sovereign" and "NATURE hath made men so equal":** The Hobbes quotations are from Hobbes (1651), Ch. 21 and Ch. 13, respectively.

98 **"In our time, he is much neglected":** Hume's criticism of Hobbes is quoted in Tuck (1989), Part III.

99 **". . . for men being all the workmanship":** Locke as quoted in Locke (1690), §6; see also Laslett (1988).

100 **"Though the Earth," "For 'tis *Labour*," "The nature [of property]," and "A *State* also of *Equality*":** The following Locke quotations are from Locke (1690), §§ 27, 40, 193 and 4, respectively.

102 **Rousseau's Social Contract:** Rousseau (1755, 1762).

104 **"It is certain that the right"** and **"Here we must remember"**: The quotations from the *Encyclopedia* are taken from the Betts translation of Rousseau (1755b), not 2.

105 **It is possible to get a bit further with modern voting theory:** The reference to modern voting theory comes from Condorcet's jury theorem; see, for example, Nurmi (2002) and Molander and Nurmi (2002).

**The Individual and the Collective:** A background of the history of the ideas is given in Hirschman (1977) and Myers (1983).

106 **The third alternative, which would eventually become the most important:** Merton (1936), Vico (1725), von Hayek (1967) and Campbell (1974) have all contributed to this tradition.

108 **Modern Analytical Versions:** Braithwaite (1955), Hamilton (1964), Trivers (1971), Axelrod (1984) with critical commentary in Molander (1992).

109 **The other branch:** Rawls (1972), Nozick (1974).

110 **At a certain remove from the controversy:** Harsanyi (1977), Binmore (1994), (1998), (2005).

## Chapter 7: Liberalism and Inequality

115 **The Contours of Liberalism:** An introduction to the history of liberalism and the more important source texts are found in Bramsted & Melhuish (1978).

**As Anthony Arblaster states:** Arblaster (1984) offers a critical perspective of liberalism's history of ideas.

116 **Of course, individualism was not born in the 1600s:** Macfarlane (1978), Le Roy Ladurie (1975).

118 **Taxation, according to Nozick, is on a par with forced la-**

**bor:** The text is not a general analysis of Nozick's theory. It might be appropriate to point out that Nozick's argument affects his own reconstruction of the night watchman state. What such a state should encompass is in no way clear-cut; some will be satisfied with a defense that only extends to a simple Home Guard, but others might think nuclear weapons are essential. If, then, anything but the minimum option is realized, proponents of this will be subjected to forced labor, to use Nozick's own terminology.

119 **"The comparable question":** The quotation about slavery is found in Nozick (1974), p. 331.

120 **There is in fact strong tension:** Popper (1945), von Hayek (1967).

121 **The modern liberal thinker Wojciech Sadurski:** Sadurski (1985), Ch. 5.

**The economist Frank Knight once noted:** The quotation is from Knight (1923).

122 **On a global level:** Milanović (2009).

**The same kind of comparisons can be made over time:** Salary comparisons are from Mishel (2006) for the United States and Bergström & Järliden Bergström (2013) for Sweden.

123 **Among conscientious English liberals:** Trollope (1883).

**Differences between individuals are often divided:** See, for example, Letwin (ed.) (1983) passim.

124 **In his doctoral thesis:** Nilsson (2009).

**In their controversial book:** Herrnstein & Murray (1994). For critical analyses, see Heckman (1995) for a statistical discussion and Fischer et al. (1996) for a more general criticism.

**"Social and economic inequalities":** The quotation is from Rawls (1972), section 46.

125 **The long-term situation is different:** Tuomala (1990).

**Rawls's theory of justice has given rise to a number of predictable responses:** For the communitarian critique of Rawls, see Mulhall & Swift (1996); among right liberals and conservatives: Nozick (1974), Letwin (ed.) (1983); criticism of the method: Harsanyi (1977b), Binmore (1994, 1998, 2005).

127 **Harsanyi's cherry-picking among human weaknesses:** For a criticism of Harsanyi, see Sen & Williams (1982), Introduction.

128 **For the theory of expected utility:** Savage (1954), Anscombe & Aumann (1963), Pratt, Raiffa & Schlaifer (1964); for a further discussion, see Harsanyi (1977).

129 **"The spirit of the Government":** The quotation from Humboldt (1792).

**In his classic text *Democracy in America*:** de Tocqueville (1835–1840).

130 **Mill wanted to protect the individual:** Mill (1859), (1848).

**A more modern and more technical version:** Schumpeter (1943), especially Part II.

## Chapter 8: Conservatism: Inequality as a Necessity and an Asset

For an introduction to conservatism's ideas and key texts, see Muller (1997). Swedish source texts include Tingsten (1939/1966), Fredriksson (1986) and Tännsjö (2001).

135 **At first, the conclusion of the analysis:** Hirschman (1991), Boulding (1975), Keyfitz (1973). The stability of unequal distri-

butions is discussed from completely different starting points in Banerjee and Duflo (2011), Banerjee et al. (eds.) (2006) and Piketty (2000).

136 **Today's conservatives are not likely to accept slavery:** On slavery in the 1900s, see Miers (2003), who, however, uses quite a broad definition.

137 **For Plato, the end point in this process was the noble lie:** See Popper (1945) for a classic criticism.

138 **"The more divine":** The quotation is from de Maistre (1814). **The following examples taken from the great world religions:** See Collins (1998) for a broad analysis of the interplay between the religions and their surrounding communities.

**Religious Foundations: Hinduism:** General references to hinduism include Rothermund (1993), Basham (ed.) (1975) and Gandhi (1947/2001).

139 **If not for DNA profiling:** Bamshad et al. (2001).

140 **In Hinduism, the blueprint for a good society:** *The Laws of Manu* have been translated into English by Doniger & Smith (1991).

141 **"For when a priest is born" and "And when a learned priest":** The quotations are taken from *The Laws of Manu* I:99–101 and VIII:37, respectively.

144 The quotations: **"My kingdom,"** John 18:36; **"Render unto Caesar,"** Matthew 22:21, Mark 12:17, Luke 20:25; **"Let every soul ...,"** Rom. 13:1–2; **"For this cause ...,"** Rom. 13:6–7.

145 **The gospel of Paul is more developed:** On the problematic figure of Paul, see Eisenman (1997).

146 **As Christianity grew in the Roman Empire:** The Christian conflict between the prohibition against murder and serving in the imperial army is discussed by Lane Fox (1986), passim.

**This unstable equilibrium between spiritual and secular power:** On Pope Gregory VII, see Berman (1983), Ch. 2.

147 **The Old Testament is a heterogeneous text:** For the Sumerian origin of the Song of Solomon, see Kramer (1981), Ch. 33.

148 **In this sense, the legitimation of slavery:** The quotation about Noah is taken from Gen. 9:20–27.
*Noah's curse:* Haynes (2002).

150 **Early Jewish commentators:** Braude (1997). Origen's homilies on Genesis and Exodus and Augustine's *The City of God* are cited in Haynes (2002).
**Noah's curse was used:** For the use of Noah's curse as a justification of the nobility's position, see Freedman (1999), Ch. 4.

151 **The relationship between an age-old legacy and legitimacy:** For Christianity's changes to the Ten Commandments, see Ex. 20:4 (repeated in Ex. 34:17) for the original version. The quotation is from Matt. 5:18.

152 **Religious Foundations: Islam:** General references that are made to Islam come from Gellner (1981) and Crone (2004).

153 **Modern researchers have challenged this idea:** Crone (2004), Berkey (2003).
**There are many parallels between Islam and Hinduism:** on Al-Biruni, see Crone (2004), p. 342.
**Typically, modern introductions to Hinduism:** Chaudhuri (1979), p. 27.
**"Do they distribute the mercy" and "That is the bounty of Allah":** The quotations from the Koran are taken from 43:32 and 62:4, respectively.

154 **To the extent that divine intervention is needed:** Crone (2003), Ch. 17.
**As for slavery:** Braude (2003).

155 **Historically speaking, the Muslim slave trade:** For the slave trade during hajj, see Miers (2003), Ch. 7.

156 **"[. . .] it must immediately occur to them":** Hume's quotation is from Hume (1739–40), Book III, Part II, Section III. Barry (1965), not U.

157 **Otherwise, the standard conservative argument:** de Maistre (1819), Burke is quoted from Muller (1997), Introduction.

158 **When history verges on myth:** On South Africa's archaeology during apartheid, see Hall (1990).
   **Somewhat surprisingly:** de Maistre as a utilitarian, quoted in Muller (1997), Introduction.

159 **One basis for conservatism's attitude to redistribution:** On unforeseen consequences, see Merton (1936).

161 **These politics have become most pronounced:** For the American right's ideological development, see Gelin (2012).

## Chapter 9: Social Democracy and Inequality

165 **"People of the same trade":** The Smith quotation is from Smith (1776), Book I, Ch. X, Part II.
   **In this endless bid for more power, larger companies will have more influence than smaller ones:** Ghemawat (1990).

169 **A traditional social-democratic strategy:** Meghir & Palme (2005), Björklund & Jäntti (2009).
   **The second key component to a social-democratic strategy:** Nordén (2005).

170 **The indirect effect of a social security system:** On the impact of unions, see Visser & Checchi (2009).

171 **Arthur Okun summarized this trade-off problem:** Okun (1975).

The connection between equality and economic development is complicated: On the connection between distribution and economic development, see Voitchovsky (2009).

172 These three basic solutions—deductions, untaxed transfers, and taxed transfers, respectively—may yield the same
result: On the true size of the American welfare state, see
Howard (1997).

More important, public spending: There is a large and in part
contradictory body of literature on the relationship between
the public sector and economic development, for example
Agell et al. (1995), Agell et al. (1997), Atkinson (1995), Barro
(1991), Cashin (1995), Hansson & Henrekson (1994), Katz et
al. (1983), Koester & Kormendi (1989), Landau (1983), Levine
& Renelt (1992), Levine & Zervos (1993), Ram (1986), and
Slemrod (1995).

The rules that govern unemployment insurance: Carling et
al. (2001), health insurance: Johansson & Palme (2002), and
pensions: Gruber & Wise (eds.) (1999).

174 If you turn the question over to Frans de Waal: de Waal
(1996).

A consistent observation: Jordahl (2009).

175 The second step in the argument: Modern research on trust
and social capital gained momentum with Putnam's book
*Making Democracy Work* from 1992, which in turn built on
Edward Banfield's study *The Moral Basis of a Backward Society*
from 1958. A relatively early reference is also Coleman (1990),
chapter 12. One of Putnam's most quoted essays is "Bowling
Alone: America's declining social capital" from 1995. An
expanded version in book-form is Putnam (2000). The summary in the text are taken from Putnam (2001).

176 **The strength of these observations varies:** Wilkinson
    (2005), Wilkinson & Pickett (2009).
    **Most investigations into the connection between trust and
    the economic growth rate:** On the connection between trust
    and economic growth, see Bjørnskov (2009).
177 **The World Bank:** The study can be found in World Bank
    (2006).


## Chapter 10: Closing the Book

183 **But following Camus:** Camus (1942).

# BIBLIOGRAPHY

Agell, J., P. Englund, J. Södersten (1995): Svensk skattepolitik i teori and praktik. 1991 års skattereform (Swedish Tax Policy in Theory and Practice. Tax Reform in 1991). Fritzes, Stockholm.

Agell, J., T. Lindh, H. Ohlsson (1997): "Growth and the Public Sector: A critical review essay," *European Journal of Political Economy* 13, 33–52.

Anscombe, F. J., R. J. Aumann (1963): "A Definition of Subjective Probability," *Annals of Mathematical Statistics* 34, 199–205.

Arblaster, A. (1984): *The Rise and Decline of Western Liberalism.* Basil Blackwell Publishers, Oxford.

Arrow, K. (1950): "A Difficulty in the Concept of Social Welfare," *Journal of Political Economy* 58 (4).

——— (1965): *Aspects of the Theory of Risk Bearing.* Yrjö Jahnssonin Saatio, Helsinki.

——— (1971): *Essays on the Theory of Risk Bearing.* Markham, N.Y.

Atkinson, A. B. (1983): *The Economics of Inequality.* 2 ed. Oxford University Press, Oxford.

——— (1995): "The Welfare State and Economic Performance," *National Tax Journal* 48, 171–98.

Atkinson, A. B., F. Bourguignon (2000): *Handbook of Income Distribution*. Vol. 1. North-Holland, Amsterdam.

Axelrod, R. (1984): *The Evolution of Cooperation*. Basic Books, N.Y.

Bamshad, M., et al. (2001): "Genetic Evidence on the Origin of Indian Caste Populations," Genome Research 11: 994–1004.

Banerjee, A., E. Duflo (2011): *Poor Economics: A Radical Rethinking of the Way to Fight Global Poverty*. Public Affairs, N.Y.

Banerjee, A. et al. (eds.) (2006): *Understanding Poverty*. Oxford University Press, Oxford.

Banfield, E. C. (1958): *The Moral Basis of a Backward Society*. Free Press, Glencoe, Ill.

Barro, R. (1991): "Economic Growth in a Cross Section of Countries," *Quarterly Journal of Economics* 106, 407–43.

Barry, B. (1965): *Political Argument*. Routledge & Kegan Paul, London.

Barton, R. A., Dunbar, R.I.M. (1997): "Evolution of the Social Brain," in Whiten & Byrne (1997).

Basham, E. L. (ed.) (1975): *A Cultural History of India*. Oxford University Press, Oxford and Delhi.

Bekar, C. T., Reed, C. G. (2009): *Risk, Asset Markets and Inequality: Evidence from Medieval England*. Discussion Paper on Economic and Social History, University of Oxford, no. 79, October 2009.

Bellman, R. E., Kalaba, R. E. (eds.) (1964): *Selected Papers on Mathematical Trends in Control Theory*. Dover, N.Y.

Bergström, J., Järliden Bergström, Å-P. (2013): *Makteliten— klyftorna består (The Ruling Elite: Enduring divisions)*. The Swedish Trade Union Confederation, Stockholm.

Berkey, J. P. (2003): *The Formation of Islam: Religion and Society in the Near East, 600–1800*. Cambridge University Press, Cambridge.

Berman, H. J. (1983): *Law and Revolution: The formation of the Western legal tradition.* Harvard University Press, Cambridge, Mass.

Binmore, K. (1994): *Playing Fair: Game theory and the social contract,* Vol. 1. MIT Press, Cambridge, Mass.

———(1998): *Just Playing: Game theory and the social contract,* Vol. 2. MIT Press, Cambridge, Mass.

———(2005): *Natural Justice.* Oxford University Press, Oxford.

———(2007): *Does Game Theory Work? The Bargaining Challenge.* MIT Press, Cambridge, Mass.

Björklund, A., Jäntti, M. (2009): "Intergenerational Income Mobility and the Role of the Family Background," in Salverda et al. (eds.) (2009).

Bjørnskov, C. (2009): "Economic growth," in Svendsen, G. T., Svendsen, G.L.H., *Handbook of Social Capital.* Edward Elgar, Cheltenham.

Boehm, C. (1997): "Egalitarianism and Political Intelligence," in Whiten and Byrne (1997).

Boix, C. (2003): *Democracy and Redistribution.* Cambridge University Press, Cambridge.

———(2010): "Origins and Persistence of Economic Inequality," *Annual Review of Political Science* 13, 489–516.

Borgerhoff Mulder, M. et al. (2010): "Pastoralism and Wealth Inequality," *Current Anthropology* 51 (1), 35–48.

Boulding, K. (1975): "The Stability of Inequality," *Review of Social Economy,* vol. 33, 1–44.

Bourguignon, F., Morrisson, C. (2002): "Inequality Among World Citizens: 1820–1992," *American Economic Review* 92 (4), 727–44.

Bowles, S., Smith, E. A., Borgerhoff Mulder, M. (2010): "The Emer-

gence and Persistence of Inequality in Premodern Societies,"
*Current Anthropology* 51 (1), 7–17.

Braithwaite, R. B. (1955): *Theory of Games as a Tool for the Moral Philosopher.* Cambridge University Press, Cambridge.

Bramsted, E. K., Melhuish, K. J. (1978): *Western Liberalism: A History of Documents from Locke to Croce.* Longman, N.Y.

Brandolini, A., Smeeding, T. M. (2009): "Income Inequality in Richer and OECD Countries," in Salverda et al. (eds.) (2009).

Braude, B. (1997): "The Sons of Noah and the Construction of Ethnic and Geographic Identities in the Medieval and Early Modern Periods," *William and Mary Quarterly* 54 (1), 103–42.

———— (2003): "Ham and Noah: Sexuality, servitudinism and ethnicity," in *Collective Degradation: Slavery and the Construction of Race.* Proceedings of the Fifth Annual Gilder Lehrman Center International Conference at Yale University (November 7–8, 2003).

Bredemeier, H. C. (1978): "Exchange Theory," in Bottomore, T., Nisbet, R. (eds.), *A History of Sociological Analysis.* Basic Books, N.Y.

Brown, D. E. (1991): *Human Universals.* McGraw-Hill, N.Y.

Buchanan, J. (1975): *The Limits of Liberty: Between anarchy and Leviathan.* University of Chicago Press, Chicago.

Buchanan, J., Tullock, G. (1962): *The Calculus of Consent: Logical Foundations of Constitutional Democracy.* University of Michigan Press, Ann Arbor.

Burke, E. (1756): *Vindication of Natural Society.* Quoted in Muller (1997). The full text is available at oll.libertyfund.org/.

Burns, A. R. (1966): *The Pelican History of Greece.* Penguin, Harmondsworth.

Butzer, K. (1976): *Early Hydraulic Civilization in Egypt.* University of Chicago Press, Chicago.

Byrne, R. W., Whiten, A. (1997): "Machiavellian Intelligence," in Whiten and Byrne (1997).

Campbell, B. (2008): "Bench-marking Medieval Economic Development: England, Wales, Scotland, and Ireland, c.1290," *Economic History Review*, 61 (4), 896–945.

Campbell, D. T. (1974): "Evolutionary Epistemology," in Schilpp, P. A. (ed.), *The Philosophy of Karl Popper*. Open Court, La Salle, Ill.

Camus, A. (1942): *Le mythe de Sisyphe*. Gallimard, Paris. Swedish trans. *Myten om Sisyfos* (*The Myth of Sisyphus*). Bonniers, Stockholm (1947).

Carling, K., Holmlund, B., Vejsiu, A. (2001): "Do Benefit Cuts Boost Job-findings? Swedish Evidence from the 1990s," *Economic Journal* 111, no. 474, 766–90.

Cashin, P. (1995): "Government Spending and Economic Growth," *IMF Staff Papers* 42(2), 237–69.

Chaudhuri, N. C. (1979): *Hinduism: A Religion to Live By*. Oxford University Press, Delhi.

Coleman, J. S. (1990): *Foundations of Social Theory*. Harvard University Press, Cambridge, Mass.

Collins, R. (1998): *The Sociology of Religions: A Global Theory of Intellectual Change*. Belknap, Harvard, Cambridge, Mass.

Cowell, F. A. (2000): "Measurement of Inequality," in Atkinson and Bourguignon (eds.) (2000).

Crone, P. (2004): *God's Rule—Government and Islam: Six Centuries of Medieval Islamic Political Thought*. Columbia University Press, N.Y.

van Damme, E. (1986): "The Nash Bargaining Solution Is Optimal," *Journal of Economic Theory* 38 (1), 78–100.

Dehaene, S. (2003): "The Neural Basis of the Weber-Fechner Law:

A Logarithmic Number Line," *Trends in Cognitive Sciences* 7 (4), 145–47.

Doniger, W., Smith, B. K. (trans.) (1991): *The Laws of Manu*. Penguin Classics, Penguin Books, Harmondsworth.

Downs, A. (1957): *An Economic Theory of Democracy*. Harper and Row, N.Y.

Durkheim, E. (1893): *De la division du travail social*. English trans. (1933) *The Division of Labor in Society*. Free Press, N.Y.

Eisenman, R. (1997): *James the Brother of Jesus*. Faber and Faber, London.

Emlen, S. T., Oring, L. W. (1977): "Ecology, Sexual Selection, and the Evolution of Mating Systems," *Science* 197 (no. 4300), 215–23.

Evans-Pritchard, E. E. (1940): *The Nuer: A Description of the Modes of Livelihood and Political Institutions of a Nilotic People*. Clarendon Press, Oxford.

Ferreira, F.H.G., Ravallion, M. (2009): "Poverty and Inequality: The global context," in Salverda et al. (eds.) (2009).

Filmer, R. (1652): *Observations Concerning the Original of Government* [. . .], in Sommerville, J. P. (1991): *Filmer: 'Patriarcha' and other political writings*. Cambridge University Press, Cambridge.

Finley, M. (1953): *Economy and Society in Ancient Greece*. Penguin, Harmondsworth.

Fischer, C. S. et al. (1996): *Inequality by Design: Cracking the Bell Curve Myth*. Princeton University Press, Princeton, N.J.

Fisher, R., Ury, W. (1981): *Getting to Yes: Negotiating Agreement Without Giving In*. Houghton Mifflin Company, Boston. Swedish trans. *Vägen till ja*. Liber ekonomi, Malmö (1992).

Foxhall, L. (2002): "Access to Resources in Classical Greece: The Egalitarianism of the Polis in Practice," in P. Cartledge, E.

E. Cohen and L. Foxhall (eds.), *Money, Labour and Land: Approaches to the Economies of Ancient Greece.* Routledge, London.

Frankena, W. K. (1973): *Ethics.* 2 ed. Prentice-Hall, Englewood Cliffs, N.J.

Fredriksson, G. (1986): *Konservativa idéer: Pessimismens politiska filosofi (Conservative Ideas: Pessimism's Political Philosophy).* Tiden, Stockholm.

Freedman, P. (1999): *Images of the Medieval Peasant.* Stanford University Press, Stanford, Ca.

Gandhi, M. K. (1947/2001): *India of My Dreams.* Articles published by R. K. Prabhu. Navajivan Publishing House, Ahmedabad.

Garnsey, P. (1988): *Famine and Food Supply in the Graeco-Roman World: Responses to Risks and Crises.* Cambridge University Press, Cambridge.

Gelin, M. (2012): *Den amerikanska högern: Republikanernas revolution och USA:s framtid (The American Right: The Republicans' Revolution and the Future of the USA).* Natur & Kultur, Stockholm.

Gellner, E. (1981): *Muslim Society.* Cambridge University Press, Cambridge.

—— (1988): *Plough, Sword and Book: The Structure of Human History.* Collins Harvill, London.

Ghemawat, P. (1990): "The Snowball Effect," *International Journal of Industrial Organization* 8, 335–51.

Goodall, J. (1990): *Through a Window: My Thirty Years with the Chimpanzees of Gombe.* Houghton Mifflin, Boston.

Goody, J. (1983): *The Development of the Family and Marriage in Europe.* Cambridge University Press, Cambridge.

Gruber, J., Wise, D. A. (eds.) (1999): *Social Security and Retirement Around the World.* University of Chicago Press, Chicago.

Gurven, M. et al. (2010): "Domestication Alone Does Not Lead to Inequality," *Current Anthropology* 51 (1), 49–64.

Hall, M. (1990): "'Hidden Archaeology': Iron Age archaeology in Southern Africa," in Robertshaw, P., *A History of African Archaeology*. James Currey Publishers, Oxford.

Hamilton, W. (1964): "The Genetical Evolution of Social Behaviour," *Journal of Theoretical Biology* 7, 1–16.

Hansson, P., Henrekson, M. (1994): "A New Framework for Testing the Effect of Government Spending on Economic Growth and Productivity," *Public Choice* 81, 381–401.

Harsanyi, J. (1956): "Approaches to the Bargaining Problem Before and After the Theory of Games: A critical discussion of Zeuthen's, Hicks', and Nash's theories," *Econometrica* 24, 144–57.

—— (1977): *Rational Behavior and Bargaining Equilibrium in Games and Social Situations*. Cambridge University Press, Cambridge.

—— (1977b): "Morality and the Theory of Rational Behaviour," *Social Research* 44(4), reprinted in Sen & Williams (1982).

von Hayek, F.A. (1959): *The Constitution of Liberty*. University of Chicago Press, Chicago.

—— (1967): "The Results of Human Action but Not of Human Design," in *Studies in Philosophy, Politics and Economics*. Routledge and Kegan Paul, London.

Haynes, S. R. (2002): *Noah's Curse: The Biblical Justification of American Slavery*. Oxford University Press, N.Y.

Heckman, J. J. (1995): "Lessons from the Bell Curve," *Journal of Political Economy* 103 (5), 1091–120.

Herrnstein, R. J., Murray, C. J. (1994): *The Bell Curve: Intelligence and Class Structure in American Life*. Free Press, N.Y.

Hirschman, A. O. (1977): *The Passions and the Interests: Political Arguments for Capitalism Before Its Triumph*. Princeton University Press, Princeton, N.J.

——— (1991): *The Rhetoric of Reaction: Perversity, Futility, Jeopardy*. Belknap/Harvard University Press, Cambridge (Mass.).

Hobbes, T. (1651): *Leviathan*. Ed. with an introduction by K. R. Minogue (1974). Dent & Sons, London.

Homans, G. C. (1961): *Social Behavior: Its Elementary Forms*. Routledge and Kegan Paul, London.

Howard, C. (1997): *The Hidden Welfare State: Tax Expenditures and Social Policy in the United States*. Princeton University Press, Princeton, N.J.

Hughes, T. P. (1971): *Elmer Sperry: Inventor and Engineer*. The Johns Hopkins University Press, Baltimore.

von Humboldt, W. (1792): *Ideen zu einem Versuch, die Grenzen der Wirksamkeit des Staates zu bestimmen*. Trans. by Coulthard, J. (1854). in *The Sphere and Duties of Government (On the Limits of State Action)*. John Chapman, London.

Hume, D. (1739–40): *A Treatise of Human Nature*. Quoted from the Fontana edition of Páll S. Árdal (1962–72).

——— (1742): "Of the Original Contract," from *Essays Moral, Political, and Literary*. Library of Economics and Liberty.

Hägerström, A. (1911): *Om moraliska föreställningars sanning (On the Truth of Moral Propositions)*. Bonniers, Stockholm.

Immervoll, H., Richardson, L. (2011): "Redistribution Policy and Inequality Reduction in OECD Countries: What Has Changed in Two Decades?" OECD Social, Employment and Migration Working Papers, no. 122, OECD Publishing, Paris.

Jakab, P. L., Young, R. (2000): The Published Writings of Wilbur and Orville Wright, Smithsonian Institution Press, Washington, D.C.

Johansson, P., Palme, M. (2002): "Assessing the Effect of Public Policy on Worker Absenteeism," *Journal of Human Resources* 37 (2), 381–409.

Jordahl, H. (2009): "Economic Inequality," in Svendsen, G.T. and Svendsen, G.L.H. (eds.), *Handbook of Social Capital*. Edward Elgar, Cheltenham.

Kalai, E. (1977): "Proportional Solutions to Bargaining Situations: Interpersonal utility comparisons," *Econometrica* 45, 1623–30.

Kalai, E., Smorodinsky, M. (1975): "Other Solutions to Nash's Bargaining Problem," *Econometrica* 43, 513–18.

Katz, C. J., Mahler, V. A., Franz, M. G. (1983): "The Impact of Taxes on Growth and Distribution in Developed Capitalist Countries: A cross-national study," *American Political Science Review* 77, 871–86.

Kelly, J. (1978): *Arrow Impossibility Theorems*. Academic Press, N.Y.

Kemeny, J. G., Snell, J. L. (1976): *Finite Markov Chains*. Springer, N.Y.

Keyfitz, N. (1973): "Can Inequality Be Cured?" *The Public Interest*, vol. 33, 91–101.

Keynes, J. M. (1936): *The General Theory of Employment, Interest and Money*. Macmillan, London.

Knauft, B. B. (1991): "Violence and Society in Human Evolution," *Current Anthropology* 32, 391–428.

Knight, F. H. (1923): "The Ethics of Competition," *Quarterly Journal of Economics* 37, 579–624.

Koester, R. B., Kormendi, R. C. (1989): "Taxation, Aggregate Activity and Economic Growth: Cross-country evidence on some supply-side hypotheses," *Economic Inquiry* XXVII, 367–86.

Kohlberg, L. (1981): *Essays on Moral Development.* Harper and Row, San Francisco.

Kramer, S. N. (1981): *History Begins at Sumer.* 3 rev. ed., University of Pennsylvania Press, Philadelphia.

Kuhn, H. W., Nasar, S. (2002): *The Essential John Nash.* Princeton University Press, Princeton, N.J.

Kymlicka, W. (1990): *Contemporary Political Philosophy: An Introduction.* Oxford University Press, Oxford. Swedish trans. *Modern politisk filosofi.* Nya Doxa, Nora (1995).

Källström, C. (1979): *Identification and Adaptive Control Applied to Ship Steering.* PhD Thesis, Faculty of Engineering, LTH, Lund University, Lund.

Landau, D. (1983): "Government Expenditure and Economic Growth," *Southern Economic Journal* 49 (4), 783–92.

Lane Fox, R. (1986): *Pagans and Christians.* Viking/Penguin Books, Harmondsworth.

Laslett, P. (1988): "Introduction," in *Locke: Two Treatises of Government,* Cambridge University Press, Cambridge.

Le Boeuf, B. J. (1974): "Male-male Competition and Reproductive Success in Elephant Seals," *American Zoologist* 14, 163–76.

Lee, D. (1974): "Introduction," in Plato. *The Republic.* 2 rev. ed., Penguin Books, Harmondsworth.

Lekberg, P. (2002): *Lives of Axes, Landscapes of People.* PhD Thesis, Department of Archaeology and Ancient History, Uppsala University.

Le Roy Ladurie, E. (1975): *Montaillou, village occitan de 1294 à 1324.* Éditions Gallimard, Paris. Swedish trans. *Montaillou: En fransk by 1294–1324 (Montaillou: A French village 1294–1324).* Atlantis, Stockholm (1980).

Letwin, W. (ed.) (1983): *Against Equality: Readings on Economic and Social Policy*. Macmillan Press, London.

Levine, R., Renelt, D. (1992): "A Sensitivity Analysis of Cross-country Regressions," *American Economic Review* 82, 942–63.

Levine, R., Zervos, S. J. (1993): "What Have We Learnt About Policy and Growth from Cross-country Regressions," *American Economic Review* 83, Papers and Proceedings, 426–30.

Lindert, P. H. (2000): "Three Centuries of Inequality in Britain and America," in Atkinson and Bourguignon (eds.) (2000).

Lindström, S. (1927): *De besegrade* (*The Vanquished*). Gebers, Stockholm.

Locke, J. (1690): *Two Treatises of Government*. Ed. by P. Laslett (1960). Cambridge University Press, Cambridge.

Macfarlane, A. (1978): *The Origins of English Individualism: The Family, Property and Social Transition*. Basil Blackwell Publishers, Oxford.

Mackie, J. L. (1977): *Ethics: Inventing Right and Wrong*. Penguin Books, Harmondsworth.

Maddison, A. (2001): *The World Economy: A Millennial Perspective*. OECD, Paris.

de Maistre, J. (1814): "Essai sur le principe générateur des constitutions politiques et des autres institutions humaines," quoted in Muller (1997), Introduction.

—— (1819) : *Du Pape*, Book II, Ch. X, quoted in Muller (1997), Introduction.

Malinowski, B. (1922): *Argonauts of the Western Pacific*. Routledge & Kegan Paul, London.

Mann, M. (1986): *The Sources of Social Power: Vol. I: A history of power from the beginning to A.D. 1760*. Cambridge University Press, Cambridge.

Maslow, A. (1936–1937): "The Role of Dominance in Social and Sexual Behaviour of Infra-human Primates," *Journal of Genetic Psychology* vol. 48, 261–77, 278–309, 310–38, and vol. 49, 161–98.

Mauss, M. (1923–1924): *Essai sur le don, forme et raison de l'échange dans les sociétés archaïques*. L'Année Sociologique, 2e série. English trans. (1954) *The Gift: Forms and functions of exchange in archaic societies*. Cohen and West, London.

Mayer, A. J. (1981): *The Persistence of the Old Regime: Europe to the Great War*. Pantheon Books, N.Y.

Mayr, O. (1969): *Zur Frühgeschichte der technischen Regelungen*. Oldenbourg, München/Wien. English trans. *The Origins of Feedback Control*. MIT Press, Cambridge, Mass. (1970).

McNeill, W. H. (1976): *Plagues and Peoples*. Anchor/Doubleday, Garden City. Swedish trans. *Farsoterna i historien*. Gidlunds, Stockholm (1985).

Meghir, C., Palme, M. (2005): "Educational Reform, Ability, and Family Background," *American Economic Review* 95 (1), pp. 414–24.

Merton, R. J. (1936): "The Unanticipated Consequences of Purposive Social Action," *American Sociological Review* 1 (6), pp. 894–904.

Meyer, D. J., Meyer, J. (2006): "Measuring Risk Aversion," *Foundations and Trends in Microeconomics* 2(2), 107–203 (reprinted by Now Publishers, Hanover, MA).

Miers, S. (2003): *Slavery in the Twentieth Century: The Evolution of a Global Problem*. Altamira Press, Walnut Creek, CA.

Milanović, B. (2006): "An Estimate of Average Income and Inequality in Byzantium Around Year 1000," *Review of Income and Wealth* 52, 449–70.

———— (2009): *Global Inequality of Opportunity—How Much of Our Income Is Determined at Birth?* Mimeo, The World Bank, Washington, D.C., February 2009.

Milanović, B., Lindert, P. H., Williamson, J. G. (2007): *Measuring Ancient Inequality.* NBER Working Paper 13550, Cambridge, Mass. Updated version, The World Bank's home page, econ.worldbank.org/projects/inequality.

Mill, J. S. (1848): *Principles of Political Economy with Some of Their Applications to Social Philosophy.* Internet ed. www.econlib.org /library/Mill/mlP.html.

———— (1859): *On Liberty.* Cited from the 2002 Modern Library edition, Random House, N.Y.

Mishel, L. (2006): "CEO-to-worker Pay Imbalance Grows," *Economic Snapshots*, June 21, 2006, Economic Policy Institute, Washington, D.C.

Molander, P. (1984): "Pangloss Paradigm," *Tvärsnitt (Cross Section)* 3/1984.

———— (1992): "The Prevalence of Free Riding," *Journal of Conflict Resolution* 36 (4), 756–71.

Molander, P., Nurmi, H. (2002): *På spaning efter folkviljan (In Search of the People's Will).* SNS Förlag, Stockholm.

Moore, G. E. (1903): *Principia Ethica.* Cambridge University Press, Cambridge.

Morrisson, C. (2000): "Historical Perspectives on Income Distribution: The case of Europe," in Atkinson & Bourguignon (eds.) (2000).

Mueller, D. (1989): *Public Choice II.* A revised edition of Public Choice. Cambridge University Press, Cambridge.

Mulhall, S., Swift, A. (1996): *Liberals and Communitarians.* 2 ed. Blackwell Publishers, Oxford.

Muller, J. Z. (ed.) (1997): *Conservatism: An Anthology of Social and Thought from David Hume to the Present.* Princeton University Press, Princeton, N.J.

Murdock, G. P., White, D. R. (1980): "Standard Cross-cultural Sample," in Barry, H., Schlegel, A. (eds.), *Cross-cultural Samples and Codes.* University of Pittsburgh Press, Pittsburgh.

Myers, M. (1983): *The Soul of Modern Economic Man.* University of Chicago Press, Chicago.

Nash, J. (1950): *Noncooperative Games.* PhD Thesis, Department of Mathematics, Princeton University. Reprinted as Ch. 6 in Kuhn and Nasar (2002).

Nicholas of Cusa (2010). *De Concordantia Catholica libri tres.* Translated by Kevin Gallagher. The Witherspoon Institute, Princeton, N.J.

Nilsson, P. (2009): *Essays on Social Interactions and the Long-term Effects of Early-Life Conditions.* PhD Thesis, Department of Economics, Uppsala University.

Nordén, C. J. (2005): *Riskgruppsutjämning—viktigare än progressivitet (Equalization Between Risk Groups: More important than progressiveness).* Background report to the Social Security Investigation. Ministry of Health and Social Affairs, Stockholm.

Nozick, R. (1974): *Anarchy, State, and Utopia.* Basic Books, N.Y.

Nurmi, H. (2002): *Voting Procedures Under Uncertainty.* Springer Verlag, Berlin.

OECD (2011): *Divided We Stand: Why Inequality Keeps Rising.* OECD, Paris.

Ok, E. (1998): "Inequality Averse Collective Choice," *Journal of Mathematical Economics* 30, 301–21.

Okun, A. (1975): *Equality and Efficiency: The Big Trade-Off.* The Brookings Institution, Washington, D.C.

Olson, M. (1965): *The Logic of Collective Action: Public Goods and the Theory of Groups*. Harvard University Press, Cambridge, Mass.

Ordeshook, P. (1992): *A Political Theory Primer*. Routledge, N.Y.

Osborne, M. J., Rubinstein, A. (1990): *Bargaining and Markets*. Academic Press, N.Y.

Osborne, R. (1992): "'Is it a Farm?': The Definition of Agricultural Sites and Settlements in Ancient Greece," in Wells, B. (ed.), *Agriculture in Ancient Greece: Proceedings of the Seventh International Symposium at the Swedish Institute of Athens*. Oxbow Books, Oxford.

Parkinson, R. B. (1991): *Voices from Ancient Egypt*. British Museum Press, London.

Piaget, J. (1932): *Le jugement moral chez l'enfant*. Librairie Félix Alcan, Paris. English trans. (1960) *Moral Judgement of the Child*. Routledge & Kegan Paul, London.

Piketty, T. (2000): "Theories of Persistent Inequality and Intergenerational Mobility," Ch. 8 in Atkinson & Bourguignon (2000).

Popper, K. (1945): *The Open Society and Its Enemies: Volume One: The Spell of Plato*. Routledge & Kegan Paul, London.

Pratt, J. W. (1964): "Risk Aversion in the Small and in the Large," *Econometrica* 32 (1–2), 83–98.

Pratt, J. W., H. Raiffa, R. Schlaifer (1964): "The Foundations of Decision Making Under Uncertainty," *American Statistical Association Journal* 59, 353–75.

Prior, A. N. (1960): "The Autonomy of Ethics," *Australasian Journal of Philosophy* 38, 199–206.

Putnam, R. D. et al. (1992): *Making Democracy Work: Civic traditions in modern Italy*. Princeton University Press, Princeton. Swedish trans. *Den fungerande demokratin*. SNS Förlag, Stockholm (1996).

—— (1995): "Bowling Alone: America's Declining Social Capital," *Journal of Democracy*, January 1995, 65–78.

—— (2000): *Bowling Alone: The Collapse and Revival of American Community*. Simon & Schuster, N.Y. Swedish trans. *Den ensamme bowlaren*. SNS Förlag, Stockholm (2006).

—— (2001): "Social capital: Measurement and Consequences," *Canadian Journal of Policy Research* 2, 41–51.

Raiffa, H. (1982): *The Art and Science of Negotiation*. Harvard University Press, Cambridge, Mass.

Ram, R. (1986): "Government Size and Economic Growth: A new framework and some evidence from cross-section and time-series data," *American Economic Review* 76 (1), 191–203.

Rawls, J. (1971): *A Theory of Justice*. Belknap/Harvard University Press, Cambridge, Mass.

Riker, W. H. (1962): *Theory of Political Coalitions*. Yale University Press, New Haven.

Rothermund, D. (1993): *An Economic History of India: From Pre-Colonial Times to 1991*. 2 ed. Routledge, London.

Rousseau, J.-J. (1755): *Discours sur l'origine et les fondements de l'inégalité parmi les hommes*. English trans. with an introduction by M. Cranston (1984), *Discourse on Inequality*, Penguin Books, Harmondsworth.

—— (1755b): *Discours sur l'économie politique*. English trans. with an introduction and notes by Christopher Betts (1999), *Discourse on Political Economy and The Social Contract*. Oxford University Press, Oxford.

—— (1762): *Du contrat social*. English trans. with an introduction by M. Cranston (1968), *The Social Contract*. Penguin Books, Harmondsworth. Swedish trans. *Om samhällsfördraget eller Statsrättens grunder*. Natur & Kultur, Stockholm (2009).

Rubinstein, A. (1982): "Perfect Equilibrium in a Bargaining Model," *Econometrica* 50, 97–109.

Sabine, G. H., Thorson, T. L. (1973): *A History of Political Theory.* 4 ed. Dryden Press, Hinsdale, Ill.

Sadurski, W. (1985): *Giving Desert Its Due: Social Justice and Legal Theory.* D. Reidel Publishing Company, Dordrecht.

Sahlins, M. (1972): *Stone Age Economics.* Tavistock Publications, London.

Salverda, W., Nolan, B., Smeeding, T. M. (eds.) (2009): *The Oxford Handbook of Economic Inequality.* Oxford University Press, Oxford.

Sandmo, A. (2014): "The Principal Problem in Political Economy: Income Distribution in the History of Economic Thought," in Atkinson, A.B. & Bourguignon, F. *Handbook of Income Distribution*, 2 ed.

Savage, L. J. (1954): *Foundations of Statistics.* Wiley, N.Y.

Scarr, C. (ed.) (2009): *The Human Past: World prehistory and the development of human societies.* 2 ed. Thames & Hudson, N.Y.

Scheidel, W. (2010): "Human Development and Quality of Life in the Long Run: The Case of Greece." Mimeo, Stanford University.

Schjelderup-Ebbe, T. (1922): "Beiträge zur Psychologie des Haushuhns" ("Contributions on the Psychology of Poultry"), *Zeitschrift für Psychologie* (*Journal of Psychology*) 88, 225–52.

Schumpeter, J. A. (1943): *Capitalism, Socialism and Democracy.* New ed. with an introduction by Tom Bottomore (1976). George Allen and Unwin, London.

Schurz, G. (1997): *The Is-Ought Problem: An Investigation in Philosophical Logic.* Kluwer, Dordrecht.

Searle, J. (1964): "How to Derive 'Ought' From 'Is,'" *Philosophical*

*Review* 73, reprinted in Hudson, W. D. (1969): *The Is-ought Question*. Macmillan Press, London.

Selander, S. (1926): *Staden and andra dikter (The City and Other Poems)*. Bonnier, Stockholm.

Sen, A. (1985): *Commodities and Capabilities*. North-Holland, Amsterdam.

—— (1992): *Inequality Reexamined*. Russell Sage Foundation/ Harvard University Press, Cambridge, Mass.

—— (2009): *The Idea of Justice*. Belknap/Harvard University Press, Cambridge, Mass.

Sen, A., Williams, B. (eds.) (1982): *Utilitarianism and Beyond*. Cambridge University Press, Cambridge.

Service, E. R. (1975): *Origins of the State and Civilization: The Process of Cultural Evolution*. Norton, N.Y.

Shenk, M. et al. (2010): "Intergenerational Wealth Transmission Among Agriculturalists," *Current Anthropology* 51 (1), 65–83.

Shubik, M. (1954): "Do the Fittest Necessarily Survive?" in *Readings in Game Theory and Political Behaviour*. Doubleday, N.Y.

Slemrod, J. (1995): "What Do Cross-country Studies Teach About Government Involvement, Prosperity and Economic Growth?" *Brookings Papers on Economic Activity* 1995 (2), 373–431.

Smith, A. (1776): *An Inquiry Into the Nature and Causes of the Wealth of Nations*, Vol. 1. Quotations from the Glasgow Edition (1981) of the *Works and Correspondence*.

Smith, E. A. et al. (2010): "Wealth Transmission and Inequality Among Hunter-gatherers," *Current Anthropology* 51 (1), 19–34.

—— (2010b): "Reply," *Current Anthropology* 51 (1), 119–26.

Soffer, O. (1985): *The Upper Paleolithic of the Central Russian Plain*. Academic Press, Orlando.

Soltow, L., van der Zanden, J.-L. (1998): *Income and Wealth In-*

*equality in the Netherlands, 16th–20th Century.* Het Spielhuis, Amsterdam.

Sophocles, trans. E. H. Plumptre (2001): *Antigone.* The Harvard Classics. New York: P. F. Collier & Son, 1909–14; Bartleby .com. www.bartleby.com/8/6/. (Accessed February 10, 2016.)

Stanton, G. R. (1990): *Athenian Politics c. 800–500 BC: A source-book.* Routledge, London.

Strauss, L., Cropsey, J. (eds.) (1987): *History of Political Philosophy.* 3 ed. University of Chicago Press, Chicago.

Ståhl, I. (1972): *Bargaining Theory.* EFI, Stockholm School of Economics, Stockholm.

——— (1994): The Rubinstein and Ståhl Bargaining Models: A comparison and an attempt at a synthesis. EFI Research Paper 6535, Stockholm School of Economics, Stockholm.

Sussmann, N. (2008): *Incomes, Inequality and Social Mobility in Late Medieval Paris.* Mimeo, Hebrew University, Jerusalem.

Taçon, P., Chippindale, C. (1994): "Australia's Ancient Warriors: Changing depictions of fighting in the rock art of Arnhem Land, N.T.," *Cambridge Archaeological Journal* 4, 211–48.

Tännsjö, T. (2001): *Konservatismen (Conservatism).* Bilda Förlag, Stockholm.

Thomas, H. (1997): *The Slave Trade: The Story of the Atlantic Slave Trade: 1440–1870.* Touchstone, N.Y.

Thomson, W. (2010): "Introduction," in Thomson, W. (ed.) (2010).

Thomson, W. (ed.) (2010): *Bargaining and the Theory of Cooperative Games: John Nash and beyond.* Edward Elgar, Cheltenham.

Tingsten, H. (1939) : *De konservativa idéerna (Conservative Ideas).* Bonniers, Stockholm. New ed. Aldus/Bonniers (1966).

Tobin, J. (2003): *To Conquer the Air: The Wright Brothers and the Great Race for Flight.* Free Press, N.Y.

de Tocqueville, A. (1835–40/1990): *De la démocratie en Amerique (On Democracy in America).* Swedish trans. *Om demokratin i Amerika.* Atlantis, Stockholm (1997).

Trivers, R. (1971): "The Evolution of Reciprocal Altruism," *Quarterly Review of Biology* 46 (1), 35–57.

Trollope, A. (1883): *Autobiography,* quoted from Bramsted & Melhuish (1978).

Tuck, R. (1989): *Hobbes.* Oxford University Press, Oxford.

Tuomala, M. (1990): *Optimal Income Tax and Redistribution.* Clarendon Press, Oxford.

Udehn, L. (1996): *The Limits of Public Choice: A Sociological Critique of the Economic Theory of Politics.* Routledge, London.

Ullman-Margalit, E. (1977): *The Emergence of Norms.* Clarendon Press, Oxford.

Vico, G. (1725): *Scienza nuova.* English trans. from 3 Ed. (1744), Bergin, T. G., Fisch, M. H. *The New Science of Giambattista Vico.* Cornell University Press, Ithaca, N.Y.

Visser, J., Checchi, D. (2009): "Inequality and the Labor Market: Unions," in Salverda et al. (eds.) (2009).

Voitchovsky, S. (2009): "Inequality and Economic Growth," in Salverda et al. (eds.) (2009).

Voltaire, F.-M. A. de (1759): *Candide, ou l'optimisme.* Swedish trans. *Candide eller Optimismen (Candide or Optimism).* Forum, Stockholm (1979).

de Waal, F. (1996): *Good Natured: The Origins of Right and Wrong in Humans and Other Animals.* Harvard University Press, Cambridge, Mass.

——(2005): *Chimpanzee Politics: Power and Sex Among Apes.* 25th anniversary edition of the original 1980 book. Johns Hopkins University Press, Baltimore.

Whiten, A., Byrne, R. W. (eds.) (1997): *Machiavellian Intelligence II: Extensions and Evaluations.* Cambridge University Press, Cambridge.

Wilkinson, R. G. (2005): *The Impact of Inequality.* The New Press, N.Y.

Wilkinson, R. G., Pickett, K. (2009): *The Spirit Level.* Penguin Books, Harmondsworth. Swedish trans. *Jämlikhetsanden.* Karneval förlag, Stockholm.

Wittfogel, K. A. (1957): *Oriental Despotism: A Comparative Study of Total Power.* Yale University Press, New Haven.

World Bank (2007): *World Development Report 2008: Agriculture for Development.* World Bank, Washington, D.C.

Wright, O. (1913): "How We Made the First Flight," *Flying.* December 1913, reprinted in Jakab, P. L., Young, R., (2000): *The Published Writings of Wilbur and Orville Wright.* Smithsonian Institution Press, Washington, D.C.

Young, P. (1993): "An Evolutionary Model of Bargaining," *Journal of Economic Theory* 59 (1), 145–68.

Zeuthen, F. (1930): *Problems of Monopoly and Economic Warfare.* Routledge, London.

## ABOUT THE AUTHOR

The recipient of the 2016 Essay Prize from the Swedish Academy, **PER MOLANDER** is the author of numerous reports, articles, and books about political philosophy and policy. He has consulted for the World Bank, the Organization for Economic Co-operation and Development, the European Commission, and the Swedish government. He lives in Uppsala, Sweden.